MUSIC
SWEET POETRY

A verse anthology compiled by

John Bishop

Drawings by Edmond X. Kapp

If music and sweet poetry agree,
As they must needs, the sister and the brother ...
RICHARD BARNFIELD

Thames Publishing
London

CONTENTS

ILLUSTRATIONS

The front cover illustration, 'Ludovic', is owned by Sir Kenneth Clark and is currently in Huddersfield Art Gallery. 'At the piano' is owned by Miss Helen Kapp, 'Wind quartet' by Mrs de Peyer, and 'Violin' by the London Philharmonic Orchestra.

INTRODUCTION

Women, sex, railways, cricket, the sea, death, travel, war, 'tough' characters, science, the Industrial Revolution: all have been the subject of recent verse anthologies. Rather surprisingly there seems not to have been one about music, whose popularity has grown so enormously in the last twenty-five years. There have, of course, been several prose-only or prose-and-verse anthologies on the subject: Charles Sayle edited an enjoyable collection in 1897, and in more recent years there have been wide-ranging miscellanies by Eric Blom and Antony Hopkins, and that of music criticism by Norman Demuth.

It soon becomes obvious when you begin to comb the bookshelves that before the present century few British poets showed any pronounced interest in music — at least in their verse; musical imagery in poems about other subjects is, of course, quite frequently found. Several of the poems used by the Elizabethan madrigalist and lutenist composers were 'about' music and the pleasure and solace it brought to life; but communing with their lutes, as they were wont, they wrote rather subjectively. Preoccupied with their lachrymose thoughts, they did not provide objective comment and reportage, though we must not forget the several Elizabethan composers and poets who wrote commendatory verses as prefaces to collections of their madrigals, church and instrumental music. Morrison Comegys Boyd's splendid study *Elizabethan Music and Musical Criticism* reprints several of these affectionate but, for the most part, poetically undistinguished and parochial pieces.

In the seventeenth and eighteenth centuries, odes to St Cecilia and to Music were popular, Dryden's (set to music by Handel) being perhaps the best. Many of the odes were intended for music — and show it; Dr Brady's words, used by Purcell for his 1692 ode, are a typical example. Even Pope nodded when he addressed himself to the task, falling back on some conventional mythological fancies.

With the exception of Coleridge and Leigh Hunt, early nineteenth-century poets showed little interest. It is not until we come to Hardy and Swinburne that we find a love of music clearly revealed in a poet's work. In recent years, Siegfried Sassoon, W. H. Auden (very knowledgeably and wittily), James Reeves, James Kirkup, Christopher Hassall, John Heath-Stubbs, Richard Church, Martin Bell, Margaret Stanley-Wrench, Julian Cooper, and Paul Jennings have written about music with perception and affection.

St Cecilia is the subject of several recent poems, including that by Auden (Blessed Cecilia, appear in visions/To all musicians, appear and inspire/Translated Daughter, come down and startle/Composing mortals with immortal fire) so vividly set to music by Benjamin Britten; it is not reproduced here since it is so closely married to the music.

Of course, not all the poems included are directly about music: music is sometimes just the catalyst that sets off the poetic fantasy — Keith Douglas's *Military Symphony* is a good example.

In making my choice — limited to about one hundred and fifty chosen from nearly twice that number — I have tried to approach the subject on the widest possible front. Alas, jazz is poorly represented because I have come across so few good poems written by British poets exploring the rich potentiality of this field of musical activity (plenty of interesting poems have, of course, been written to be recited *to* jazz). Otherwise, apart from the general estimates of the place music has in life and its potent evocative powers, there are tributes and subjective reactions to composers and particular works, aspects of street-music and music in the home, the concert hall, the opera house and the church: even a little humour, and such delightful fancies — in their very different ways — as Leigh Hunt's imaginary concert and Aubrey Beardsley's quaint period-piece.

The anthologist's dilemma, as chronic here as ever, is what to leave out. One or two candidates proved too expensive in copyright fees; one or two others were rather too long for a book of this size. Several poems were omitted because I consider them too familiar, although few of the hoary anthology favourites are in fact about music: even the devotee of poetry would be hard put to name more than Campion's *When to her lute Corinna sings*, Wyatt's *Awake my lute*, the Dryden ode and *Alexander's Feast*, Browning's *A Tocatta of Galuppi's* and *Master Hugues*, Milton's *At a solemn music*, Shakespeare's *Orpheus with his lute*, the *Free Thoughts* of Charles Lamb, and Yeats's *The fiddler of Dooney*.

Edmond Kapp's line-drawings do much to enhance the anthology. Throughout his long career as an artist he was compulsively drawn to musical subjects. These 12 drawings are representative of hundreds showing professionals at their business and amateurs at their pleasure.

The great reward of compiling this book has been to bring to light a host of deserving, largely unfamiliar treasures, a paean of loving affirmations of the joy that music brings — music which, to quote Plato, 'gives soul to the universe, wings to the mind, flight to the imagination, a charm to sadness, gaiety and life to everything'.

February 1983   JOHN BISHOP

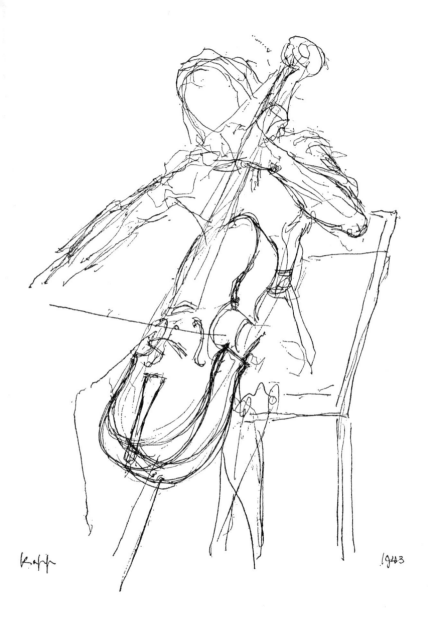

Kopp   1943

MUSIC'S POWER: HOMAGE TO ST CECILIA

To a Friend in Praise of Music and Poetry

If music and sweet poetry agree,
    As they must needs, the sister and the brother,
Then must the love be great 'twixt thee and me,
    Because thou lov'st the one and I the other.
Dowland to thee is dear whose heavenly touch
    Upon the lute doth ravish human sense,
Spenser to me, whose deep conceit[1] is such
    As passing all conceit needs no defence.
Thou lov'st to hear the sweet melodious sound
    That Phoebus' lute, the queen of music, makes,
And I in deep delight am chiefly drowned,
    When as himself to singing he betakes.
One god is god of both, as poets feign,
One knight loves both, and both to thee remain.

RICHARD BARNFIELD

Music

When the last note is played and void the hall
I sometimes think that then music begins.
Scattered on chairs lie horns and violins,
The harp droops silent, standing by the wall;
On the live ear no sounds of music fall,
The organ sleeps, coiled in its branching wood.
But this deep soundlessness is music's food,
This quiet is big with thunder; if I call
At once a thousand spirits rave and cry,

---

[1] thought

Those instruments gape, quivering helplessly,
With strangled voices vibrant and wild they sigh;
And I can hear in that great solitude
Madness and grief, not the smooth harmony
That presently, subdued, they'll sing to me.

W. J. TURNER

Music

When music sounds, gone is the earth I know,
And all her lovely things even lovelier grow;
Her flowers in vision flame, her forest trees
Lift burdened branches, stilled with ecstasies.

When music sounds, out of the water rise
Naiads whose beauty dims my waking eyes,
Rapt in strange dreams burns each enchanted face,
With solemn echoing stirs their dwelling-place.

When music sounds, all that I was I am
Ere to this haunt of brooding dust I came;
While from Time's woods break into distant song
The swift-winged hours, as I hasten along.

WALTER DE LA MARE

Katt. '26

Recorder Duet

Music's Empire

First was the world as one great cymbal made
Where jarring winds to infant nature played;
All music was a solitary sound,
To hollow rocks and murmuring fountains bound.

Jubal first made the wilder notes agree,
And Jubal tunèd Music's jubilee;
He called the echoes from their sullen cell,
And built the organ's city where they dwell.

Each sought a consort in that lovely place,
And virgin trebles wed the manly bass,
From whence the progeny of numbers new
Into harmonious colonies withdrew;

Some to the lute, some to the viol went,
And others chose the cornet eloquent.
These practising the wind, and those the wire,
To sing man's triumphs, or in Heaven's quire.

Then music, the mosaic of the air,
Did of all these a solemn noise prepare,
With which she gained the empire of the ear,
Including all between the earth and sphere.

Victorious sounds! yet here your homage do
Unto a gentler conqueror than you;
Who, though he flies the music of his praise,
Would with you Heaven's hallelujahs raise.

ANDREW MARVELL

The Penny Whistle

The new moon hangs like an ivory bugle
In the naked frosty blue;
And the ghylls of the forest, already blackened
By Winter, are blackened anew.

The brooks that cut up and increase the forest,
As if they had never known
The sun, are roaring with black hollow voices
Betwixt rage and a moan.

But still the caravan-hut by the hollies
Like a kingfisher gleams between:
Round the mossed old hearths of the charcoal-burners
First primroses ask to be seen.

The charcoal-burners are black, but their linen
Blows white on the line;
And white the letter the girl is reading
Under that crescent fine;

And her brother who hides apart in a thicket,
Slowly and surely playing
On a whistle an old nursery melody
Says far more than I am saying.

EDWARD THOMAS

A Song to the Lute in Music

Where griping griefs the heart would wound,
   And doleful dumps the mind oppress,
There music with her silver sound
   With speed is wont to send redress:
Of troubled minds, in every sore,
Sweet music hath a salve in store.

In joy it makes our mirth abound,
   In woe it cheers our heavy sprites;
Bestraughted heads relief hath found
   By music's pleasant sweet delights;
Our senses all — what shall I say more? —
Are subject unto music's lore.

The gods by music have their praise;
   The life, the soul therein doth joy;
For, as the Roman poet says,
   In seas whom pirates would destroy,
A dolphin saved from death most sharp
Arion playing on his harp.

O heavenly gift that rules the mind,
   Even as the stern doth rule the ship!
O music, whom the gods assign'd
   To comfort man whom cares would nip!
Since thou both man and beast do'st move,
What beast is he will thee disprove?

RICHARD EDWARDS

Sweet Harmony

Lorenzo   How sweet the moonlight sleeps upon this bank!
            Here will we sit, and let the sounds of music
            Creep in our ears: soft stillness and the night
            Become the touches of sweet harmony.
            Sit, Jessica: look how the floor of heaven
            Is thick inlaid with patines of bright gold:
            There's not the smallest orb which thou behold'st
            But in his motion like an angel sings,
            Still quiring to the young-eyed cherubins:
            Such harmony is in immortal souls;
            But whilst this muddy vesture of decay
            Doth grossly close it in, we cannot hear it.
            Come, ho, and wake Diana with a hymn!
            With sweetest touches pierce your mistress' ear,
            And draw her home with music.
Jessica   I am never merry when I hear sweet music.
Lorenzo   The reason is, your spirits are attentive:
            For do but note a wild and wanton herd,
            Or race of youthful and unhandled colts,
            Fetching mad bounds, bellowing, and neighing loud,
            Which is the hot condition of their blood;
            If they but hear perchance a trumpet sound,
            Or any air of music touch their ears,
            You shall perceive them make a mutual stand,
            Their savage eyes turn'd to a modest gaze
            By the sweet power of music: therefore the poet
            Did feign that Orpheus drew trees, stones, and floods;
            Since nought so stockish, hard, and full of rage,
            But music for the time doth change his nature.
            The man that hath no music in himself,
            Nor is not moved with concord of sweet sounds,
            Is fit for treasons, stratagems, and spoils;
            The motions of his spirit are dull as night,

And his affections dark as Erebus:
Let no such man be trusted. — Mark the music . . .

Nerissa   It is your music, madam, of the house.
Portia   Nothing is good, I see, without respect;
             Methinks it sounds much sweeter than by day.
Nerissa   Silence bestows that virtue on it, madam.

WILLIAM SHAKESPEARE

Preface to a Musician

Do you know how to begin?
Take the string or the reed,
And grow old with it in your hand.
Wake in the night
To feel if you hold it with freedom.
Let your mornings be heavy
With wonder if your suppleness remains;
And the day a long labour,
And the years a fear of stiffness.
Then perhaps towards the end,
Time frosting your joints,
You will make music,
Shake hills,
Drag men in their multitudes
As the moon drags the sea.

RICHARD CHURCH

In Commendation of Music

When whispering strains do softly steal
With creeping passion through the heart,
And when at every touch we feel
Our pulses beat and bear a part;
  When threads can make
  A heartstring shake,
  Philosophy
  Can scarce deny
The soul consists of harmony.

When unto heavenly joy we feign
Whate'er the soul affecteth most,
Which only thus we can explain
By music of the wingèd host,
  Whose lays we think
  Make stars to wink,
  Philosophy
  Can scarce deny
Our souls consist of harmony.

O lull me, lull me, charming air,
My senses rock with wonder sweet;
Like snow on wool thy fallings are,
Soft, like a spirit's, are thy feet:
  Grief who need fear
  That hath an ear?
  Down let him lie
  And slumb'ring die
And change his soul for harmony.

WILLIAM STRODE

On Hearing Mrs Woodhouse Play the Harpsichord

We poets pride ourselves on what
   We feel, and not what we achieve;
The world may call our children fools,
   Enough for us that we conceive.
A little wren that loves the grass
Can be as proud as any lark
   That tumbles in a cloudless sky,
Up near the sun, till he becomes
   The apple of that shining eye.

So, lady, I would never dare
   To hear your music ev'ry day;
With those great bursts that send my nerves
   In waves to pound my heart away;
And those small notes that run like mice
Bewitched by light; else on those keys —
   My tombs of song — you should engrave:
'My music, stronger than his own,
   Has made this poet my dumb slave'.

W. H. DAVIES

Fragment to Music

No, Music, thou art not the 'food of Love',
Unless Love feeds upon its own sweet self,
Till it becomes all Music murmurs of.

PERCY BYSSHE SHELLEY

For a Musician

Many musicians are more out of order than their instruments; such as are so, may by singing this Ode become reprovers of their untunable affections: they who are better tempered, are hereby remembered what music is most acceptable to God, and most profitable to themselves.

What helps it those,
  Who skill in song have found,
Well to compose
  Of disagreeing notes,
By artful choice,
  A sweetly pleasing sound,
To fit their voice,
  And their melodious throats?
What helps it them
  That they this cunning know,
If most condemn
  The way in which they go?

What will he gain
  By touching well his lute,
Who shall disdain
  A grave advice to hear?
What from the sounds
  Of organ, fife, or lute,
To him rebounds,
  Who doth no sin forbear?
A mean respect,
  By tuning strings he hath,
Who doth neglect
  A rectifièd path.

Therefore, O Lord!
  So tunèd let me be

Unto Thy Word
  And Thy ten-stringèd law,
That in each part
  I may thereto agree,
And feel my heart
  Inspired with loving awe;
He sings and plays
  The song which best Thou lovest,
Who does and says
  The things which Thou approvest.

Teach me the skill
  Of him whose heart assuaged
Those passions ill
  Which oft afflicted Saul;
Teach me the strain
  Which calmeth minds enraged,
And which from vain
  Affections doth recall:
So to the choir
  Where angels music make,
I may aspire
  When I this life forsake.

GEORGE WITHER

15

Dame Musike

And so to a chambre full solacious[1]
Dame Musike wente with La Bell Pucell.[2]
All of jasper with stones precious
The rofe was wrought curiously and well;
The windowes glased mervailously to tell;
With clothe of tissue in the richest maner
The walles were hanged hye and circuler.

There sate Dame Musike with all her minstralsy,
As taboures, trumpettes, with pipes melodious,
Sakbuttes, organs, and the recorder swetely,
Harpes, lutes, and crowddes[3] right delicious,
Symphans,[4] doussemers,[5] with claricymbales[6] glorious,
Rebeckes, claricordes, eche in their degre,
Dide sitte aboute their ladyes mageste.

Before Dame Musike I dide knele adowne,
Sayenge to her, 'O faire lady pleasaunt,
Your prudence reineth most hye in renowne,
For you be ever right concordant
With perfite reason, whiche is not variaunt:
I beseche your grace with all my diligence
To instructe me in your noble science'.

'It is', she saide, 'right gretely prouffitable,
For musike doth sette in all unite
The discorde thinges which are variable,
And devoideth[7] mischefe and grete iniquite;
Where lacketh musicke there is no pleinte,
For musike is concorde and also peace:
Nothinge without musike maye well encreace.

---

[1] delightful   [2] the Fair Maiden   [3] fiddles   [4] instruments in general
[5] dulcimers   [6] clavicymbals   [7] expels

'The seven sciences in one monacorde[1]
Eche upon other do full well depende;
Musike hath them so set in concorde
That all in one maye right well extende;
All perfite reason they do so comprehende
That they are waye and perfite doctrine
To the joye above, whiche is celestine.

'And yet also the perfite physike,
Which appertaineth well to the body,
Doth well resemble unto the musike;
Whan the inwarde intrailes tourneth contrary,
That nature cannot werke directly,
Than doth physike the partes interiall
In ordre set to their originall.

'And musike selfe it is melodious
To rejoyce the eeres and confort the braine,
Sharpinge the wittes with sounde solacious,
Devoidinge bad thoughtes which dide remaine;
It gladdeth the herte also well certaine,
Lengthe the life with dulcet armony;
It is good recreacion after study'.

She commaunded her minstrelles right anone to play
Mamours,[2] the swete and the gentill daunce;
With La Bell Pucell that was faire and gaye
She me recommaunded with all pleasaunce
To daunce true mesures without variaunce.
O Lorde God, how gladly than was I,
So far to daunce with my swete lady.

By her propre[3] hande soft as ony silke
With due obeisaunce I dide her than take.

1 harmony   2 'My love'   3 own

Her skinne was white as whalles bone or milke;
My thought was ravisshed; I might not aslake
My brenninge[1] hert: she the fire dide make.
These daunces truely Musike hath me tought:
To lute or daunce but it availed nought.

For the fire kindled and waxed more and more;
The dauncinge blewe it with her beaute clere;
My hert sekened[2] and began waxe sore:
A minute six houres, and six houres a yere,
I thought it was, so hevy was my chere;
But yet for to cover my great love aright,
The outwarde countenance I made gladde and light.

STEPHEN HAWES: from *The Pastime of Pleasure*

On Music

Many love music but for music's sake,
Many because her touches can awake
Thoughts that repose within the breast half dead,
And rise to follow where she loves to lead.
What various feelings come from days gone by!
What tears from far-off sources dim the eye!
Few, when light fingers with sweet voices play
And melodies swell, pause, and melt away,
Mind how at every touch, at every tone,
A spark of life hath glistened and hath gone.

WALTER SAVAGE LANDOR

[1] burning   [2] sickened

On Music

When thro' life unblest we rove,
　Losing all that made life dear,
Should some notes we used to love,
　In days of boyhood, meet our ear,
Oh! how welcome breathes the strain!
　Wakening thoughts that long have slept:
Kindling former smiles again
　In faded eyes that long have wept.

Like the gale, that sighs along
　Beds of oriental flowers,
Is the grateful breath of song,
　That once was heard in happier hours;
Fill'd with balm, the gale sighs on,
　Though the flowers have sunk in death;
So when pleasure's dream is gone,
　Its memory lives in Music's breath.

Music, oh how faint, how weak,
　Language fades before thy spell!
Why should Feeling ever speak,
　When thou canst breathe her soul so well?
Friendship's balmy words may feign,
　Love's are ev'n more false than they;
Oh! 'tis only Music's strain
　Can sweetly soothe, and not betray.

THOMAS MOORE

Music

I have been urged by earnest violins
And drunk their mellow sorrows to the slake
Of all my sorrows and my thirsting sins.
My heart has beaten for a brave drum's sake.
Huge chords have wrought me mighty: I have hurled
Thuds of God's thunder. And with old winds pondered
Over the curse of this chaotic world,
With low lost winds that maundered as they wandered.

I have been gay with trivial fifes that laugh;
And songs more sweet than possible things are sweet;
And gongs, and oboes. Yet I guessed not half
Life's sympathy till I had made hearts beat,
And touched Love's body into trembling cries,
And blown my love's lips into laughs and sighs.

WILFRED OWEN

To Musique, to Becalme his Fever

Charm me asleep, and melt me so
    With thy Delicious Numbers;
That being ravisht, hence I goe
    Away in easie slumbers.
        Ease my sick head,
        And make my bed,
Thou Power that canst sever
        From me this ill:
        And quickly still:
        Though thou not kill
            My Fever.

Thou sweetly canst convert the same
    From a consuming fire,
Into a gentle-licking flame,
    And make it thus expire.
        Then make me weep
        My paines asleep;
And give me such reposes,
        That I, poore I,
        May think, thereby,
        I live and die
            'Mongst Roses.

Fall on me like a silent dew,
    Or like those Maiden showrs,
Which, by the peepe of day, doe strew
    A Baptime o're the flowers.
        Melt, melt my paines,
        With thy soft straines;
That having ease me given,
        With full delight,
        I leave this light;
        And take my flight
            For Heaven.

ROBERT HERRICK

A Cry to Music

Speak to us, Music, for the discord jars;
The world's unwisdom brings or threatens Death.
Speak, and redeem this misery of breath
With that which keeps the stars
Each to her point in the eternal wheel
That all clear skies reveal.

Speak to us; lift the nightmare from us; sing.
The screams of chaos make the daylight mad.
Where are the dew-drenched mornings that we had
When the lithe lark took wing?
Where the still summers, when more golden time
Spoke to us, from the lime?

Though these be gone, yet, still, Thy various voice
May help assuage the pangs of our distress,
May hush the yelling where the fiends rejoice,
Quiet the sleepless, making sorrow less.
Speak, therefore, Music; speak.
Calm our despair; bring courage to the weak.

Ah, lovely Friend, bring wisdom to the strong,
Before a senseless strength has all destroyed.
Be sunlight on the night of brooding wrong.
Be form among the chaos of the void.
Be Music; be Thyself; a prompting given
Of Peace, of Beauty waiting, and sin shriven.

JOHN MASEFIELD

The Gods' Consort

What, have the gods their consort sent from heaven,
    To charm my senses with heaven's harmony?
Care they for me, of all my joys bereaven?
    Send they heaven's choir to make me melody,
    Blessing me with music's felicity?
If it be so, great may your godheads be,
And greater still to ease my misery.

Methinks I hear Amphion's warbling strings,
    Arion's harp distilling silv'ring sound,
Orpheus' mean lute, which all in order brings,
    And with soul-pleasing music doth abound,
    Whilst that old Phemius softly plays the ground.
O sweet consort, great may your comfort be,
And greater still to ease my misery.

ANON., 17th century

Chromatic Tunes

Can doleful notes to measured accents set
Express unmeasured griefs that time forget?
No, let chromatic tunes, harsh without ground,
    Be sullen music for a tuneless heart;
Chromatic tunes most like my passions sound,
    As if combined to bear their falling part.
Uncertain certain turns, of thoughts forecast
Bring back the same, then die, and, dying, last.

ANON., 17th century

Phoebus and Pan

To his sweet lute Apollo sung the motions of the spheres,
The wondrous order of the stars whose course divides the years,
    And all the mysteries above.
    But none of this could Midas move,
    Which purchased him his ass's ears.

Then Pan with his rude pipe began the country-wealth to advance,
To boast of cattle, flocks of sheep, and goats on hills that dance,
    With much more of this churlish kind,
    That quite transported Midas' mind,
    And held him rapt as in a trance.

This wrong the God of Music scorned from such a sottish judge,
And bent his angry bow at Pan, which made the piper trudge.
    Then Midas' head he so did trim,
    That every age yet talks of him
    And Phoebus' right-revenged grudge.

ANON., 17th century

To Musick

Begin to charme, and as thou stroak'st mine eares
With thy enchantment, melt me into tears.
Then let thy active hand scu'd o're thy Lyre:
And make my spirits frantick with the fire.
That done, sink down into a silv'rie straine;
And make me smooth as Balme, and Oile againe.

ROBERT HERRICK

Sonnet

Music to hear, why hear'st thou music sadly?
Sweets with sweets war not, joy delights in joy:
Why lov'st thou that which thou receiv'st not gladly,
Or else receiv'st with pleasure thine annoy?
If the true concord of well-tuned sounds,
By unions married, do offend thine ear,
They do but sweetly chide thee, who confounds
In singleness the parts that thou should'st bear.
Mark how one string, sweet husband to another,
Strikes each in each by mutual ordering;
Resembling sire and child and happy mother,
Who, all in one, one pleasing note do sing:
  Whose speechless song, being many, seeming one,
  Sings this to thee: 'Thou single wilt prove none.'

WILLIAM SHAKESPEARE

Music's Tragedy

Had birds no season for their precious songs,
  What would we call them but a common pest?
Since Music's now a manufactured thing,
  Potted and churned in every house we pass —
Think of the birds, how they more wisely sing.

That Paradise we dreamed of years ago,
  When Music, rarely heard, was thought divine,
Is for the 'Damned', and not the 'Happy Blest';
  Since, fed by force, with Music cheapened so —
Is there no quiet place to sleep or rest?

W. H. DAVIES

Solace to my Thoughts

Music, dear solace to my thoughts neglected,
Music, time sporter to my most respected,
Sound on, sound on, thy golden harmony is such
That whilst she doth vouchsafe her ebon lute to touch,
By descant numbers I do nimbly climb from Love's secluse
Unto his courts, where I in fresh attire attire my Muse.

I do compare her fingers' swift resounding
Unto the heavens' spherical rebounding.
Hark, hark, she sings! No forced but breathing sound I hear,
And such the concord diapasons she doth rear,
As when the immortal god of nature from his seat above
First formed words all, and fairly it combined, combined by Love.

Divine Apollo, be not thou offended
That by her better skill thy skill's amended.
Scholars do oft more lore than masters theirs attain,
Though thine the ground, all parts in one though she contain,
Yet mayst thou triumph that thou hast a scholar only one
That can her lute to thine, and to thy voice her voice attone.

ANON., 17th century

Upon her Voice

Let but thy voice engender with the string,
And Angels will be borne, while thou dost sing.

ROBERT HERRICK

A Tune

A foolish rhythm turns in my idle head
As a wind-mill turns in the wind on an empty sky.
Why is it when love, which men call deathless, is dead,
That memory, men call fugitive, will not die?
Is love not dead? yet I hear that tune if I lie
Dreaming awake in the night on my lonely bed,
And an old thought runs with the old tune in my head
As a wind-mill turns in the wind on an empty sky.

ARTHUR SYMONS

Music Comes

Music comes
Sweetly from the trembling string
When wizard fingers sweep
Dreamily, half asleep;
When through remembering reeds
Ancient airs and murmurs creep,
Oboe oboe following,
Flute answering clear high flute,
Voices, voices — falling mute,
And the jarring drums.

At night I heard
First a waking bird
Out of the quiet darkness sing . . .

Music comes
Strangely to the brain asleep!

And I heard
Soft, wizard fingers sweep
Music from the trembling string,
And through remembering reeds
Ancient airs and murmurs creep;
Oboe oboe following,
Flute calling clear high flute,
Voices faint, falling mute,
And low jarring drums;
Then all those airs
Sweetly jangled — newly strange,
Rich with change . . .
Was it the wind in the reeds?
Did the wind range
Over the trembling string;
Into flute and oboe pouring
Solemn music; sinking, soaring
Low to high,
Up and down the sky?
Was it the wind jarring
Drowsy far-off drums?

Strangely to the brain asleep
Music comes.

JOHN FREEMAN

Lines Composed in a Concert-room

Nor cold, nor stern, my soul! yet I detest
   These scented Rooms, where, to a gaudy throng
Heaves the proud Harlot her distended breast,
   In intricacies of laborious song.

These feel not Music's genuine power, nor deign
   To melt at Nature's passion-warbled plaint;
But when the long-breathed singer's uptrilled strain
   Bursts in a squall — they gape for wonderment.

Hark! the deep buzz of Vanity and Hate!
   Scornful, yet envious, with self-torturing sneer
My lady eyes some maid of humbler state,
   While the pert Captain, or the primmer Priest,
   Prattles accordant scandal in her ear.

O give me, from this heartless scene released,
   To hear our old Musician, blind and grey,
(Whom stretching from my nurse's arms I kissed)
   His Scottish tunes and warlike marches play,
By moonshine, on the balmy summer-night,
   The while I dance amid the tedded hay
With merry maids, whose ringlets toss in light.

Or lies the purple evening on the bay
Of the calm glossy lake, O let me hide
   Unheard, unseen, behind the alder-trees,
For round their roots the fisher's boat is tied,
   On whose trim seat doth Edmund stretch at ease,
And while the lazy boat sways to and fro,
   Breathes in his flute sad airs, so wild and slow,
That his own cheek is wet with quiet tears.

But O, dear Anne! when midnight wind careers,
And the gust pelting on the out-house shed
   Makes the cock shrilly in the rainstorm crow,
   To hear thee sing some ballad full of woe,
Ballad of ship-wreck'd sailor floating dead,
   Whom his own true-love buried in the sands!
Thee, gentle woman, for thy voice remeasures
Whatever tones and melancholy pleasures
   The things of Nature utter; birds or trees,
Or moan of ocean-gale in weedy caves,
Or where the stiff grass mid the heath-plant waves,
   Murmur and music thin of sudden breeze.

SAMUEL TAYLOR COLERIDGE

A Singing Lesson

Far-fetched and dear-bought, as the proverb rehearses,
Is good, or was held so, for ladies: but nought
In a song can be good if the turn of the verse is
   Far-fetched and dear-bought.

As the turn of a wave should it sound, and the thought
Ring smooth, and as light as the spray that disperses
Be the gleam of the words for the garb thereof wrought.

Let the soul in it shine through the sound as it pierces
Men's hearts with possession of music unsought;
For the bounties of song are no jealous god's mercies,
   Far-fetched and dear-bought.

ALGERNON CHARLES SWINBURNE

F is for Fiddler

What an enchanted world is this,
   What music I have heard: and when
I hear these Master fiddlers play,
   I ask — 'Are these not marvellous men?'
So, since such men command the sweetest sounds,
   I'll have no fear to leave my solitude
Of woods and fields,
   And join the human multitude;
To hear a Master's hand express
The very soul and tenderness
   Heard when a pigeon's cooing there;
To hear him make the robin sob again,
   In Autumn, when the trees go bare;
Till — touching one lamb-bleating string —
We leap the Winter into Spring.

W. H. DAVIES

The Spinet

My heart's an old Spinet with strings
   To laughter chiefly tuned, but some
   That Fate has practised hard on, dumb,
They answer not whoever sings.
The ghosts of half-forgotten things
   Will touch the keys with fingers numb,
   The little mocking spirits come
And thrill it with their fairy wings.

A jingling harmony it makes
  My heart, my lyre, my old Spinet,
And now a memory it wakes
  And now the music means 'forget',
And little heed the player takes
  How e'er the thoughtful critic fret.

ANDREW LANG

Piano

Softly, in the dusk, a woman is singing to me;
Taking me back down the vista of years, till I see
A child sitting under the piano, in the boom of the tingling strings
And pressing the small, poised feet of a mother who smiles as she
  sings.

In spite of myself, the insidious mastery of song
Betrays me back, till the heart of me weeps to belong
To the old Sunday evenings at home, with winter outside
And hymns in the cosy parlour, the tinkling piano our guide.

So now it is vain for the singer to burst into clamour
With the great black piano appassionato. The glamour
Of childish days is upon me, my manhood is cast
Down in the flood of remembrance, I weep like a child for the
  past.

D. H. LAWRENCE

The Composer

All the others translate: the painter sketches
A visible world to love or reject;
Rummaging into his living, the poet fetches
The images out that hurt and connect,

From Life to Art by painstaking adaption,
Relying on us to cover the rift;
Only your notes are pure contraption,
Only your song is an absolute gift.

Pour out your presence, a delight cascading
The falls of the knee and the weirs of the spine,
Our climate of silence and doubt invading;

You alone, alone, imaginary song,
Are unable to say an existence is wrong,
And pour out your forgiveness like a wine.

W. H. AUDEN

Ye Sacred Muses

Ye sacred Muses, race of Jove,
Whom Music's love delighteth,
Come down from crystal heavens above
To earth where Sorrow dwelleth
In mourning weeds, with tears in eyes.
Tallis is dead, and Music dies.

ANON., 17th century

Saint Cecilia

And so, night after night,
From the ranked citadel of tubes, the graduated
Throats of song, the organ's rising flutes —
Like hollow reed-stems, bound with wax and twine,
That pour shrill music to the listening hills,
While over them a satyr's hairy mouth
Trembles — praise went up to the blue
And drooping silver-dusted petals of
The heavens' hanging rose;
In fantasy and fugue, static and carved
Upon the streaming moments, like the vine
With symmetry of frond and tendril turned
In stone, on a stone porch. And my pale hands,
With cool and delicate fingers, frail as spires
Of some faint water-plant, whose grace
No lover might emprison,
Division made upon the ivory keys.

And yet my body was a pool,
Tremulous, bottomless, where through the dark
Plunged ever down and down that silver fish
My silent heart — though still went up
A voice from hand exact, and calculating
Eye, and weighed in leverage of the forearm's poise.

And the Moon stooping to the female curve
Of the high unglazed window through the night,
Whispered her pagan fancies:
'O my wise daughter, who have made this choice,
Desiring never lover's touch, but only
Abstract caress of song, and that cold flame
That sweeps around you, flickering, springing from
The dancing rhythms of your own clear blood —

34

Oh you shall turn and find
My secret island fane, embowered in woods
Of murmuring pine, the smooth white pillars of
My sacred house, served only by sweet choir
Of virgin girls, white-veiled, who feed my stags
And wreathe their silver horns, or graced by the dance
And glimmering limbs of clear-eyed boys,
And sexless tone of their high-sounding voices:
Puellae et pueri integri. . . .'
So spoke, and rose, and soared
Up to her midnight throne,
Showing the Palatine, and smoke of torches borne
By obscene, cruel revellers, and swathed forms lurking
Beneath expectant arches.

But now another visitor has come
To hear my dove-winged chords and silver scale,
And three nights in the shadow he has stood
Erect, yet with bowed head, and six wings furled
About his bare and splendid body;
Long hair like small blue flames swept back above
His lucid brows, and great eyes deep with love;
Sword girt about his shining loins, — sentinel
Of God's high eastern watch-tower, set to challenge
The radiant Sun with words, when fiery hoov'd
His steeds beat up the dawn.

He brings me roses that are red like pain.

JOHN HEATH-STUBBS

35

Music Divine

Music divine, proceeding from above,
Whose sacred subject oftentimes is love,
In this appears her heavenly harmony,
Where tuneful concords sweetly do agree.
And yet in this her slander is unjust,
To call that love which is indeed but lust.

ANON., 17th century

Dance Band

Swim with the stream! Sleep as you swim! Let the wave take you!
However loud they play, my saxophones will never wake you
For they are in your dream and you in theirs;
My beat is in your blood whose pulse it shares;
My drums are in your veins, close as your heart;
Your flanks are moulded by the waves they part;
This stream's the moving shadow of your thigh.
Dance and forget to die, forget to die!

I am New York aware of Africa and something lost:
I am two exiles, Judah and the jungle, Broadway-crossed:
Nostalgia spangled, fear-of-the-dark striped with brown
    laughter:
Now in a lighted room, defying *Before* and *After*,
That pair who tap on the window-panes and burrow through the
    bone-thin rafter.

A. S. J. TESSIMOND

The Songs

Continuous, a medley of old pop numbers —
Our lives are like this. Three whistled bars
Are all it takes to catch us, defenceless
On a District Line platform, sullen to our jobs,
And the thing stays with us all day, still dapper, still Astaire,
Still fancy-free. We're dreaming while we work.
Be careful, keep afloat, the past is lapping your chin.
South of the Border is sad boys in khaki
In 1939. And *J'attendrai* a transit camp,
Tents in the dirty sand. Don't go back to Sorrento.
Be brisk and face the day and set your feet
On the sunny side always, the sunny side of the street.

MARTIN BELL

Walking Home on St Cecilia's Day

It is sublime adjustment: now
The only home for a deep sunk spine
Raising blood cordial, the plain wine
Of the bored. They can never trespass enough

Against us, who use their surly right
Of making the world hateful. The rose
Foot is in the clay and the catgut clothes
The notes of ink. On our backs the freight

Is never less and the pack sores rub,
But these are scabs of scarab, Atlas' welts
Where the whole world has hung or else
No single blade of grass could stand up.

The packed authority is in one glance.
The injustice of delight! All that is made
Makes this ventriloquist's serenade —
Words to sing, beautiful impermanence.

And feeling my death in me, I walk home,
Rehearsing wrongly Mozart's own congruity.
Thus I say to the gatepost, see
I could be drunk and not fall to this huge drone.

It is the maker's gift, mechanic sound,
Which they say can analyse to God.
But here is hunger where we would feel greed;
We can learn it, a miracle on the ground.

But it still won't make tomorrow other than
Another day of chafing, shaving, sitting still:
Nodules on noses grow, pet cats get killed,
The lush and smooth upstage the scrag and thin.

But I know now as I charge my batteried heart
With thirty years' unhappiness on end,
There is a practice of music which befriends
The ear — useless, impartial as rain on desert —

And conjures the listener for a time to be happy,
Making from this love of limits what he can,
Saddled with Eden's gift, living in the reins
Of music's huge light irresponsibility.

PETER PORTER

For the Death of Anton Webern Particularly

Sunday gardening, hoeing, trying to think of nothing but
hoeing — so that this at least can be an exercise in the true sense —
nevertheless I can think of little but the death of Anton Webern.
I just happened to read it. It just happened to be Webern.
One has ferreted out and written up at length how the Weberns
went out to dine some night with their daughter and their
(unbeknown to them) blackmarketeer of a son-in-law, shortly
after the American occupation. The G.I. agent provocateur went out
to block any escape. Just at that moment, in the black back yard,
the fragile Webern, out to puff a gift cigar, collided
with the decoy who shot him by mistake. Back home, not knowing
whom he'd killed, but withered by it, this kind man died of drink.

Sunday gardening, hoeing, I turn over the worms in their beds
and am shadowed by the blackbirds. And I have to ask again from what
body-stitching those worms are sundered and picked out writhing to die,
and from what soul-harrowing that Rome of blackbirds flutters down
to drill and gut the worms with javelin beaks, and in the fold of what
wedding of body and desire in Jerusalem I am conceived and born
to offer this show. I need not ask on what Sunday God first churned
his cauldron world in such a manner that we all deal death,
not knowing that we deal it, scarcely caring, yet dying of it too
from afar — in what stew God first mixed meat of worm,
feather and beak of bird and hand of man and what bubbles
send up each in turn to do the other in. And how, the last, the notes
composed by fragile Webern survive the boil and music in the bubbles.

NATHANIEL TARN

39

A Closing Music

So music flowed for them, and left
The silence brimmed.

Music took charge that evening, and with deft
Flights into rhapsody, a clarinet
Sang of their passion — while a candle slimmed,
The window had its fingering of dark rain.

It was not music chosen to forget
The separation and the pain to come:
It caught the separation and the pain
Into the high dark of its tender dance.

Firelight and candlelight and rain were dumb
(Which often spoke their moods for them) to speak
This exaltation. Soft in stare and glance,
These waited for the music to say all.

And three times through a falling air would break
Such tenderness — such pity — of dark strings,
It could have been surmised there would befall
Something, not faced, but fingered round by doubt.

And it was death, and it was death, that things
Meant all that time. And love's one world was cleft
From top to bottom. All their lights gone out,
Their praises to the god of joy, all hymned.

Music had flowed in them. It left
The silence brimmed.

LAURENCE WHISTLER

MUSIC IN AND
OUT OF DOORS

To all Musicians

A little music, please, but let
It be smooth, dulcet,
Such as royal lovers, in the act
Of breeding future dynasties,
Commanded from strings, hautboys, flutes,
Too proud to hide their animal pursuits
From eyes pretending to ignore the fact,
While fastening on staves.

Performers, you are slaves
Even today, though Demos reigns,
And the few princes who survive
Are half-apologetic, taking pains
To ingratiate themselves with Tom, Dick
And Harry in the body politic.

You also must contrive
To look as though the pleasures of the mob
Are your delight and choice.
So glance discreetly down, give voice
To the sweet sounds that are your job,
Persuading still, as once at a king's feast,
That what is done is not the mark of the beast.

RICHARD CHURCH

To a Child at the Piano

Play the tune again; but this time
with more regard for the movement at the source of it,
and less attention to time. Time falls
curiously in the course of it.

Play the tune again; not watching
your fingering, but forgetting, letting flow
the sound till it surrounds you. Do not count
or even think. Let go.

Play the tune again; but try to be
nobody, nothing, as though the pace
of the sound were your heart beating, as though
the music were your face.

Play the tune again. It should be easier
to think less every time of the notes, of the measure.
It is all an arrangement of silence. Be silent, and then
play it for your pleasure.

Play the tune again; and this time, when it ends,
do not ask me what I think. Feel what is happening
strangely in the room as the sound glooms over
you, me, everything.

Now,
play the tune again.

ALASTAIR REID

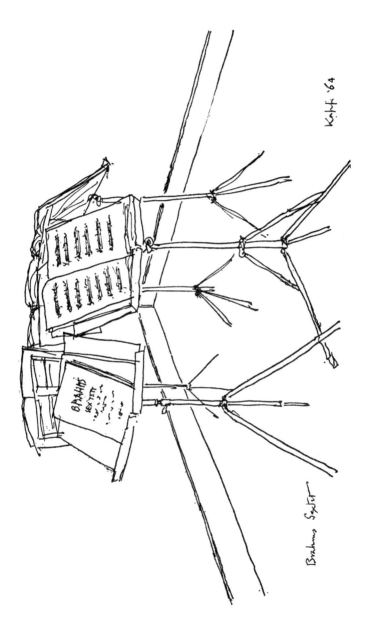

Brahms Septet

KAH '64

On a Lady Singing Lawes's Music to Milton's Ode on the Nativity

I closed my eyes, and heard your voice recall,
  Your delicate voice, exact and small and pure,
Each lovely curve and cunning interval,
  Obeying his command with instinct sure:
But caught no echo of that thunderous hymn
  From Zion's walls, where stand in burning row
The ranks of rainbow-wingèd Seraphim,
  Who loud their long uplifted trumpets blow.

Zion was silent: and I only heard
  As 'twere in dawn's dim twilight, in a wood,
The faint sweet music of a hidden bird
  Singing a private joy, not understood
By me, but strangely comforting to me,
From the deep heart of some invisible tree.

J. C. SQUIRE

The Morris Dance

Ho! who comes here along with bagpiping and drumming?
O 'tis the morris dance I see, a-coming.
  Come ladies out, come quickly!
And see about how trim they dance and trickly.
  Hey! there again! how the bells they shake it!
  Hey ho! now for our town! and take it!
Soft awhile, piper, not away so fast! They melt them.
Be hanged, knave! see'st thou not the dancers swelt them?
  Stand out awhile! you come too far, I say, in.
  There give the hobby-horse more room to play in!

ANON., 17th century

Lines to William Linley
while he Sang a Song to Purcell's Music

While my young cheek retains its healthful hues,
  And I have many friends who hold me dear,
   L —! methinks, I would not often hear
Such melodies as thine, lest I should lose
All memory of the wrongs and sore distress
  For which my miserable brethren weep!
  But should uncomforted misfortunes steep
My daily bread in tears and bitterness;
And if at Death's dread moment I should lie
  With no belovéd face at my bed-side,
To fix the last glance of my closing eye,
  Methinks such strains, breathed by my angel-guide,
Would make me pass the cup of anguish by,
  Mix with the blest, nor know that I had died!

SAMUEL TAYLOR COLERIDGE

Ballad Singers

Let not the Ballad-Singer's shrilling Strain
Amid the Swarm thy list'ning Ear detain:
Guard well thy Pocket; for these *Syrens* stand,
To aid the Labours of the diving Hand;
Confed'rate in the Cheat, they draw the Throng,
And *Cambrick* Handkerchiefs reward the Song.
But soon as Coach or Cart drives rattling on,
The Rabble part, in Shoals they backward run.
So *Jove*'s loud Bolts the mingled War divide,
And *Greece* and *Troy* retreats on either side.

JOHN GAY: from Trivia

To a Lady that Desired me I Would
Bear my Part with her in a Song

This is the prettiest motion:
Madam, th' alarums of a drum
That calls your lord, set to your cries,
To mine are sacred symphonies.

What, though 'tis said I have a voice;
I know 'tis but that hollow noise
Which, as it through my pipe doth speed,
Bitterns do carol through a reed;
In the same key with monkeys' jigs,
Or dirges of proscribed pigs,
Or the soft serenades above
In calm of night, when cats make love.

Was ever such a consort seen!
Fourscore and fourteen with fourteen!
Yet sooner they'll agree, one pair,
Than we in our Spring-Winter air;
They may embrace, sigh, kiss the rest:
Our breath knows naught but east and west.
Thus have I heard to children's cries
The fair nurse 'stil such lullabies
That well all said, for what there lay,
The pleasure did the sorrow pay.

Sure there's another way to save
Your fancy, madam; that's to have
('Tis but petitioning kind Fate)
The organs sent to Billingsgate;
Where they to that soft murm'ring choir
Shall reach you all you can admire!

Or do but hear how love-bang Kate
In pantry dark, for fridge of meat,
With edge of steel the square wood shapes,
And *Dido* to it chants or scrapes.
The merry Phaëton o' th' car
You'll vow makes a melodious jar;
Sweeter and sweeter whistleth he
To unanointed axletree;
Such swift notes he and 's wheels do run;
For me, I yield him Phoebus' son.

Say, fair commandress, can it be
You should ordain a mutiny?
For where I howl, all accents fall
As kings' harangues to one and all.

Ulysses' art is now withstood,
You ravish both with sweet and good;
Saint siren, sing, for I dare hear,
But when I ope, oh stop your ear!

Far less be 't emulation
To pass me or in trill or tone,
Like the thin throat of Philomel,
And the smart lute, who should excel,
As if her soft chords should begin,
And strive for sweetness with the pin.

Yet can I music too; but such
As is beyond all voice or touch;
My mind can in fair order chime,
Whilst my true heart still beats the time;
My soul so full of harmony,
That it with all parts can agree:
If you wind up to the highest fret,
It shall descend an eight from it,

And when you shall vouchsafe to fall,
Sixteen above you it shall call,
And yet so disassenting one,
They both shall meet an unison.

Come then, bright cherubin, begin!
My loudest music is within:
Take all notes with your skilful eyes,
Hark if mine do not sympathize!
Sound all my thoughts, and see express'd
The tablature of my large breast,
Than you'll admit that I too can
Music above dead sounds of man;
Such as alone doth bless the spheres,
Not to be reach'd with human ears.

RICHARD LOVELACE

The Quartette

Tom sang for joy and Ned sang for joy and old Sam sang for
joy;
All we four boys piped up loud, just like one boy;
All the ladies that sate with the Squire — their cheeks were all
wet,
For the noise of the voice of us boys, when we sang our Quartette.

Tom he piped low and Ned he piped low and old Sam he piped
low;
Into a sorrowful fall did our music flow;
And the ladies that sate with the Squire vowed they'd never
forget
How the eyes of them cried with delight, when we sang our
Quartette.

WALTER DE LA MARE

The Old Singer

He came to sing some olden songs
That scarcely any now remember.
He braved a night of wild December
   And tramped in pregnant with his wrongs.

He grumbled at his weight of years
And cursed the harsh, unfriendly season;
He offered all-sufficient reason
   Why future time for him meant tears.

Yet when the wight began to sing
An ancient, Carolean ditty,
He asked for no man's ruth or pity,
   But made the cottage dresser ring.

His songs for him won passing sleight
To summon vanished folk together,
Helped him forget his slender tether
   And woke a laugh that wintry night.

His far-off look and far-off smile
Welcomed dead men and women, stealing
With faint and ghostly power of healing
   To hearten him a little while.

EDEN PHILLPOTTS

The Guitarist Tunes Up

With what attentive courtesy he bent
Over his instrument;
Not as a lordly conqueror who could
Command both wire and wood,
But as a man with a loved woman might,
Inquiring with delight
What slight essential things she had to say
Before they started, he and she, to play.

FRANCES CORNFORD

Boy with a Mouth Organ

Lips hardened by winter's dumb duress
Part on this other, broader smile of youth
That masks deep shyness in its shallow kiss,
While silently behind its music laughs the mouth
Of Pan, and mourns the skull of a severer myth.

The keen and thick-fingered eyes denote
Languor, delight, astonishment or grief,
Interpreters expressive of the heart
That makes the lake dance, and the leaf.

Boy, in cupped hands hold whatever passion time invents:
Fire your tiny forges with gigantic sound, and fill
Heaven with your fierce harmonics! Inspire those instruments,
Aeolus, lyre and grove-hung harp, that now miraculously thrill
Our childhood, the toy that trembles to an ancient will!

JAMES KIRKUP

Mirth and Music

Aye, at times on summer evenings,
It was there for one sweet hour
That we met for mirth and music,
On the green beside the bower,
Ere as yet the flitting blackbird
Still'd her singing for the night,
Or the evening shed its dew-drops
In the lily's cup of white.
By ones or twos, two or one,
We sang and play'd our music
Out before the evening sun.

There were young men spry and comely
That could sound a pipe or string;
There were maidens fair and merry
That could sweetly chat or sing.
There were young men smart and witty,
There was many a maiden tongue,
With a voice in talk or laughter
All as sweet as when it sung.
By ones or twos, two or one,
We sang and play'd our music
Out before the evening sun.

Down at mill the yellow sunlight
Brightly glared on window glass,
And the red cows' sides were gilded
In the field of flow'ry grass.
And with us the sunny lands
All around were fair to see
And each beating heart was merry,
And each tongue alive with glee
As one and all, all and one,

Enjoyed the mirth and music
Out before the summer sun.

WILLIAM BARNES

Cornet Solo

Thirty years ago lying awake,
Lying awake
In London at night when childhood barred me
From livelier pastimes, I'd hear a street-band break
Into old favourites — *The Ash Grove*, *Killarney*
Or *Angels Guard Thee*.

That was the music for such an hour —
A deciduous hour
Of leaf-wan drizzle, of solitude
And gaslight bronzing the gloom like an autumn flower —
The time and music for a boy imbrued
With the pensive mood.

I could have lain for hours together,
Sweet hours together,
Listening to the cornet's cry
Down wet streets gleaming like patent leather
Where beauties jaunted in cabs to their revelry,
Jewelled and spry.

Plaintive its melody rose or waned
Like an autumn wind
Blowing the rain on beds of aster,
On man's last bed: mournful and proud it complained
As a woman who dreams of the charms that graced her,
In young days graced her.

Strange how those yearning airs could sweeten
And still enlighten
The hours when solitude gave me her breast.
Strange how they could tell a mere child how hearts may beat
    in
The self-same tune for the once-possessed
And the unpossessed.

Last night, when I heard a cornet's strain,
It seemed a refrain
Wafted from thirty years back — so remote an
Echo it bore: but I felt again
The prophetic mood of a child, too long forgotten,
Too lightly forgotten.

C. DAY LEWIS

Old Gramophone Records

(Discovered in an album at Corsham Court, England)

On these ancient disks, smooth-backed, severe,
And thick as slates, we trace the grooves
Our grandparents' needles pricked, and hear —
How far away! — the hoarse echoes of their Edwardian loves.

O, Songs Round the Piano! Edison Bell! His Master's Voice!
Those were the days when, unscratched still, with well-bred style
The plush-hung, stiff-lipped *Lieder* singer's choice
Vibrato matched her rolling eye, her bust, her topnote smile.

Here are the absurdity and brassband charm
Of Auber — *Zanetta Overture*, and Meyerbeer,
The *March from Le Prophète*; *Jerusalem
The Golden*, chorused by the Mixed Church Choir.

A gloomy contralto, Mme L. Dews,
Neighs, moos and bleats above a quailing
Pianoforte accompaniment, in *The Promise
Of Life,* and *Three Fishers Went Sailing.*

Mr John Harrison (tenor) renders
I Know a Lovely Garden — (the composer
Guy Hardelot, a *lady* to those in the know); and the splendours
And miseries of *A Love Song,* by Kaiser.

Bel canto Caruso! Carl Jörn (Kgl. Hofopernsänger)
Nobly delivers, with a voice like velvet and gold braid,
The *Preislied* from the *Meistersinger.*
Mme Amy Castles 'gives' us Gounod's *Serenade.*

Dear darling of the musicale, Dame Nellie Melba,
Promises, from her gold-signed salmon label, *Caro Nome,*
Then, in a lingering farewell, the same divine and only diva,
Emotional and rapt, laments *The Old Folks at Home.* . . .

Hurrah! the spluttering soundbox, big as a samovar,
The exotic gold and orange trumpet like a hothouse plant
Bawls out *Pale Hands I Loved Beside the Shalimar* . . .;
Patti in *La Calesera* screams; a silver band thumps out *Poet and
    Peasant.*

We smile, for we cannot explain the sadness which these voices
    cast.
And the turntable turns on a ghost of the ghosts of the past.

JAMES KIRKUP

Effect of Military Music on a Welfare-worker

Remote in the dream perspective of the street
   That, at the breaking of each winter day,
In the long diminuendoes of worn feet
   Remembers its grey story, and is grey,

A curious sound begins, fantastic sound
   That wholly alters what it hardly suits,
Till dogs are grabbed, and heads are swivelled round,
   And squealing sashes honour the recruits.

Huge and extraordinary in brass they come,
   Their great nasturtiums filling the drab air
With eulogies of glory, while the drum
   No more than stutters in the key of fear.

And as Miss Bramble lifts in studied pain
   A soapstone gaze upon the panting tubas,
Ridiculous gaiety sweeps from her brain
   All hatred of the class for which she labours;

So that this tumid moment she would stick
   At nothing you could ask her: she would gladly
Unfrock the Bishop in a limerick,
   Or put a match to Latimer and Ridley.

LAURENCE WHISTLER

Park Concert

Astounding the bucolic grass,
The bandsmen sweat in golds and reds
And put their zeal into the brass.
A glorious flustered major heads

Their sort of stationary charge.
Their lips are pursed, their cheeks get pink;
The instruments are very large
Through which they render Humperdinck.

The sailors and the parlourmaids
Both vote the music jolly good,
But do not worry if it fades
As they stroll deeper in the wood,

Where twenty French horns wouldn't stir
A leaf. The intrepid band try not
To mind the applause (as though it were
A testing fusilade of shot),

Polish their mouthpieces and cough,
Then throw their shoulders back to play
A Pomeranian march. They're off!
And Sousa scares the tits away.

JAMES MICHIE

The Musical Box

What pale, Victorian invalid, obsessed
With the dank fogs that greased the window pane,
Sent for this musical box and lightly pressed
The catch to make her pulses dance again?
Lead, Kindly Light or *Soldiers of the Queen*,
Tangles of *Rigoletto*, *Home Sweet Home* —
Echoes of melodies that once had been
Practised with fervour to a metronome.
And now, another child confined to bed,
Her trembling ringlets shorn, her fires subdued,
Lies with the same desires disquieted,
Seeking enchantment in her solitude;
Again the bright delirious hammers play
Come to the Ball, Ta-ra-ra Boom-de-ay!

JEAN KENWARD

The Military Harpist

Strangely assorted, the shape of song and the bloody man.

Under the harp's gilt shoulder and rainlike strings,
Prawn-eyed, with prawnlike bristle, well-waxed moustache,
With long tight cavalry legs, and the spurred boot
Ready upon the swell, the Old Sweat waits.

Now dies, and dies hard, the stupid, well-relished fortissimo,
Wood-wind alone inviting the liquid tone,
The voice of the holy and uncontending, the harp.

Ceasing to ruminate interracial fornications,
He raises his hands, and his wicked old mug is David's,
Pastoral, rapt, the king and the poet in innocence,

Singing Saul in himself asleep, and the ancient Devil
Clean out of countenance, as with an army of angels.

He is now where his bunion has no existence.
Breathing an atmosphere free of pipeclay and swearing,
He wears the starched nightshirt of the hereafter, his halo
Is plain manly brass with a permanent polish,
Requiring no oily rag and no Soldier's Friend.

His place is with the beloved poet of Israel,
With the wandering minnesinger and the loves of Provence,
With Blondel footsore and heartsore, the voice in the darkness
Crying like beauty bereaved beneath many a donjon,
O Richard! O king! where is the lion of England?
With Howell, Llewellyn, and far in the feral north
With the savage fame of the hero in glen and in ben,
At the morning discourse of saints in the island Eire,
And at nameless doings in the stone-circle, the dreadful grove.

Thus far into the dark do I delve for his likeness:
He harps at the Druid sacrifice, where the golden string
Sings to the golden knife and the victim's shriek.
Strangely assorted, the shape of song and the bloody man.

RUTH PITTER

The Basie Band

The beat and beat and growl of the Basie band
Swish-swish it goes
I only hope I'm there at the close.

Like tigers roaring on a stormy night
The trumpets wail
The thudding drum beats down like falling hail.

Like a jungle bird the lightly flitting flute
Sings to the roar below
Where saxophones are prowling to and fro.

Like raindrops dropping: little piano notes
So neatly falling on the keys
And the guitarist riffing gently through the trees.

Like a herd of stampeding wildebeest
The big band goes
Running before the thunder of the close.

JULIAN COOPER

Arab Music

Simply one warm night, among much warmth and many nights:
Simply bare voices and bare hands, a bare street
Strewn with the refuse of the very poor.

Them, like the first carol, the never-sung-before: in dirty robes
Transfigured, their sick eyes gleamed: simply,
Among the scurrying taxis, dark gathered Nubians.

Pure and simple their voices swung, fell, climbed
Long versatile rhetorics: their hard hands
Applauded themselves, throbbed through tense silences.
    Lean uninstructed one-man men,
Yet last in the world that still sing like a people.

Caesar's cold camp once stood here: and the stiff shapes,
Since then, of other missionaries and business men,
Embittered by grit, a mocking wind, a lying race.
Only a dim policeman cowers, now, shy and indigenous,
Among the mad trams and his madder fellows.

The song soars still, violent and vast: their history,
Daily paper, church, their nuptial bed, their narrow grave:
   All held
Between bare hands, borne on bare midnight voices.

D. J. ENRIGHT

Concert Party (Egyptian Base Camp)

They are gathering round . . .
Out of the twilight; over the grey-blue sand,
Shoals of low-jargoning men drift inward to the sound —
The jangle and throb of a piano . . . tum-ti-tum . . .
Drawn by a lamp they come
Out of the glimmering lines of their tents, over the shuffling sand.

O sing us the songs, the songs of our own land,
You warbling ladies in white.
Dimness conceals the hunger in our faces,
This wall of faces risen out of the night,
These eyes that keep their memories of the places
So long beyond their sight.

Jaded and gay, the ladies sing; and the chap in brown
Tilts his grey hat; jaunty and lean and pale,
He rattles the keys . . . some actor-bloke from town . . .
God send you home; and then *A long, long trail*;
I hear you calling me; and *Dixieland* . . .
Sing slowly . . . now the chorus . . . one by one.
We hear them, drink them; till the concert's done.
Silent, I watch the shadowy mass of soldiers stand,
Silent, they drift away, over the glimmering sand.

SIEGFRIED SASSOON

The Sitar Player

He slurs his fingers on the strings
That clang and whine in tortured chords.
No-one is talking while the sitar sings.

There is magnetism in those notes
Which veer about one selfsame chord —
Phrases repeated like a magic word.

And in between he makes such plays,
His fingers skate about the scales;
But all the time the sound of clanging stays.

The faster that his playing gets
The calmer his mind appears to be,
As if it could rise up above the melody;

Until there's hardly a gap between
The notes or between the quickening blows
The tabla player hammers on his bongos.

At last, after the cascading rush
Of counterpoint, and off-beat rhythms,
They quiet down and close it with a hush

Of sound, an echo of a theme
At the beginning. And everything they've played,
So deftly, fits together in one scheme.

JULIAN COOPER

Music in a Spanish Town (Cordoba 1936)

In the street I take my stand
with my fiddle like a gun against my shoulder,
and the hot strings under my trigger hand
shooting an old dance at the evening walls.

Each saltwhite house is a numbered tomb
its silent window crossed with blood;
my notes explode everywhere like bombs
when I should whisper in fear of the dead.

So my fingers falter, and run in the sun
like the limbs of a bird that is slain,
as my music searches the street in vain.

Suddenly there is a quick flutter of feet
and children crowd about me,
listening with sores and infected ears,
watching with lovely eyes and vacant lips.

LAURIE LEE

The Fiddler

The fiddler knows what's brewing
  To the lilt of his lyric wiles:
The fiddler knows what rueing
  Will come of this night's smiles!

He sees couples join them for dancing,
  And afterwards joining for life,
He sees them pay high for their prancing
  By a welter of wedded strife.

He twangs: 'Music hails from the devil,
    Though vaunted to come from heaven,
For it makes people do at a revel
    What multiplies sins by seven.

'There's many a heart now mangled,
    And waiting its time to go,
Whose tendrils were first entangled
    By my sweet viol and bow!'

THOMAS HARDY

The Musician

A memory of Kreisler once:
At some recital in this same city,
The seats all taken, I found myself pushed
On to the stage with a few others,
So near that I could see the toil
Of his face muscles, a pulse like a moth
Fluttering under the fine skin,
And the indelible veins of his smooth brow.

I could see, too, the twitching of the fingers,
Caught temporarily in art's neurosis,
As we sat there or warmly applauded
This player who so beautifully suffered
For each of us upon his instrument.

So it must have been on Calvary
In the fiercer light of the thorns' halo:
The men standing by and that one figure,
The hands bleeding, the mind bruised but calm,

Making such music as lives still.
And no one daring to interrupt
Because it was himself that he played
And closer than all of them the God listened.

R. S. THOMAS

At Madame Tussaud's in Victorian Years

'That same first fiddler who leads the orchestra tonight
    Here fiddled four decades of years ago;
He bears the same babe-like smile of self-centred delight,
    Same trinket on watch-chain, same ring on the hand with
      the bow.

'But his face, if regarded, is woefully wanner, and drier,
    And his once dark beard has grown straggling and gray;
Yet a blissful existence he seems to have led with his lyre,
    In a trance of his own, where no wearing or tearing had
      sway.

'Mid these wax figures, who nothing can do, it may seem
    That to do but a little thing counts a great deal;
To be watched by kings, councillors, queens, may be flattering
    to him —
    With their glass eyes longing they too could wake notes that
      appeal.'

Ah, but he played staunchly — that fiddler — whoever he was,
    With the innocent heart and the soul-touching string:
May he find the Fair Haven! For did he not smile with good
    cause?
    Yes; gamuts that graced forty years'-flight were not a small
      thing!

THOMAS HARDY

Practising the Virginals

As when a maide, taught from her mother's wing
To tune her voice unto a silver string,
When she should run, she rests; rests when should run,
And ends her lesson having now begun:
Now misseth she her stop, then in her song,
And, doing of her best, she still is wrong;
Begins again, and yet again strikes false,
Then in a chafe forsakes her virginals;
And yet within an hour she tries anew,
That with her daily pains (art's chiefest due)
She gains that charming skill, and can no less
Tame the fierce walkers of the wilderness
Than that Œagrian[1] harpist, for whose lay
Tigers with hunger pined and left their prey.

WILLIAM BROWNE

[1] Orpheus, the son of Œagrus and Calliope, according to Plato

IN THE
CONCERT HALL

Symphony

At last like a divining rod
His baton dips, and all the poised
Wrists move together and recoil,
A shuttle of slanted bows that weave a texture soon
Thickened with barely audible horns; and picking their way
Down a black labyrinth, the assembled
Listeners follow the taper of a motif lost
And glimpsed again round modulated bends, till one
By one, seduced by their own fancies,
They diverge down secret passages which lead
Them back by torturous, fantastic ways
To daylight. One reflects
'It spreads me out like small change on a counter'.
Another 'These ripples lapping towards me break
Far, far behind. I am only sitting in their way,
Yet they flow *through* me. Is it the breath of life,
Like breath in a French horn, that fills and sounds me?
Am I myself the instrument this music plays?
Its breath within me leaves a pulsing warmth
Made by the resonant pressure round my concave walls.'
And some, as the minims hang and waver by,
In fancy leap and lunge to grasp their meaning,
Like children in a field adrift with thistledown;
Others, more tranquil, on their upturned palms
Hold out a crumb of attention for the timid bird
That hovers near but is always
Hoisting itself away. Among them a girl,
By the tilted and gilded harp reminded of
'The barge she sat in', proceeds in state
Between the banks of Cydnus. The sallow man
Beside her has come to lose himself in sound
As in a wood. Propt by a tree, he grows
Aware of a hyacinth smelling of new-dug earth,

Then suddenly remembers what were best
Forgotten, and desolation like a seventh wave
Breaks quietly along the whole reach of his mind's
Defenceless shore. Shifting a foot, he jogs
His neighbour who with concentration's frown
Has waded in mid-stream and stands
Intent, up to the knees in a torrent of counterpoint,
Like a man fishing. This is he that listens,
Hearing the discourse of a master spirit
Uttered in his own terms, pure sound, the strings
And brass and that first motif like a blazing torch
Uplifted, eloquent, big with human triumph.
The word was uttered, hard to comprehend,
But who else even heard it? Only the child,
Perhaps, whose open mind was a blank
But for the moment when he saw again
The tiger-moth that flew out of his clothes
One blue, crisp, hungry morning, as he began
To dress. And once more he had caught it
Had not the brittle reverie been snapped
By his own hands which inadvertently
Conforming to the general applause
Had started clapping.

CHRISTOPHER HASSALL

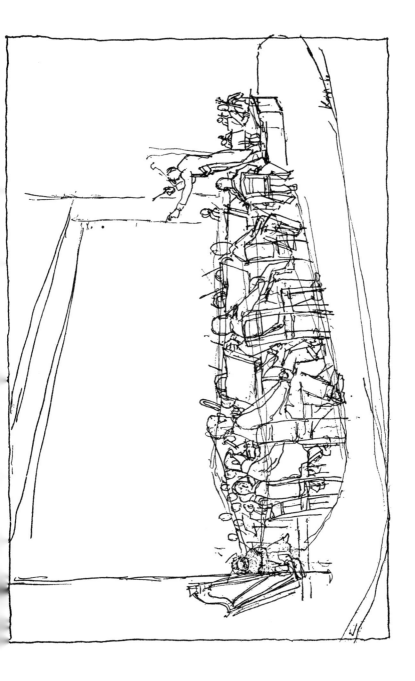

Wagner

Creeps in half wanton, half asleep,
  One with a fat wide hairless face.
He likes love-music that is cheap;
  Likes women in a crowded place;
    And wants to hear the noise they're making.

His heavy eyelids droop half-over,
  Great pouches swing beneath his eyes.
He listens, thinks himself the lover,
  Heaves from his stomach wheezy sighs;
    He likes to feel his heart's a-breaking.

The music swells. His gross legs quiver.
  His little lips are bright with slime.
The music swells. The women shiver.
  And all the while, in perfect time,
    His pendulous stomach hangs a-shaking.

RUPERT BROOKE

Concert-Interpretation (Le Sacre du Printemps)

The audience pricks an intellectual Ear . . .
Stravinsky . . . Quite the Concert of the Year!

Forgetting now that none-so-distant date
When they (or folk facsimilar in state
Of mind) first heard with hisses — hoots — guffaws —
The abstract Symphony (they booed because

Stravinsky jumped their Wagner palisade
With modes that seemed cacophonous and queer),
Forgetting now the hullabaloo they made,
The Audience pricks an intellectual ear.

Bassoons begin . . . Sonority envelops
Our auditory innocence; and brings
To Me, I must admit, some drift of things
Omnific, seminal, and adolescent.
Polyphony through dissonance develops
A serpent-conscious Eden, crude but pleasant;
While vibro-atmospheric copulations
With mezzo-forte mysteries of noise
Prelude Stravinsky's statement of the joys
That unify the monkeydom of nations.

This matter is most delicate indeed!
Yet one perceives no symptom of stampede.
The Stalls remain unruffled: craniums gleam:
Swept by a storm of pizzicato chords,
Elaborate ladies reassure their lords
With lifting brows that signify 'Supreme!'
While orchestrated gallantry of goats
Impugns the astigmatic programme-notes.

In the Grand Circle one observes no sign
Of riot: peace prevails along the line.
And in the Gallery, cargoed to capacity,
No tremor bodes eruptions and alarms.
They are listening to this not-quite-new audacity
As though it were by someone dead, — like Brahms.

But savagery pervades Me; I am frantic
With corybantic rupturing of laws.
Come, dance, and seize this clamorous chance to function
Creatively, — abandoning compunction

In anti-social rhapsodic applause!
Lynch the conductor! Jugulate the drums!
Butcher the brass! Ensanguinate the strings!
Throttle the flutes! . . . Stravinsky's April comes
With pitiless pomp and pain of sacred springs . . .
Incendiarize the Hall with resinous fires
Of sacrificial fiddles scorched and snapping! . . .

Meanwhile the music blazes and expires;
And the delighted Audience is clapping.

SIEGFRIED SASSOON

Symphony Orchestra

In the profound platform's floodlit aquarium
Quiver and brood the black, liquid plumes of a grand
Pianoforte, drowning with last wave-opened
Wing in foaming pools that overbrim each dim drum.

Triumphant brasses, golden flower trumpets, lift
Singing faces to forlorn horns faint as a hand
High-strung in harp caves. Double basses, heads inclined,
Precise and elegant as hippocampi drift

In weeds, in weaving hands that swim in violins
Like pale shoals of pointed fishes — pouncing, dancing,
Dividing, diving; pausing, nibbling, advancing
Serene on sound-currents, the concerted ocean's

Roars and whispers a sea god calms, excites, commands,
O! with deep-sounding trident in exalted hands!

JAMES KIRKUP

A Violin Concerto

Now is the focus of all hopes:
  She poises on the topmost stair.
And many-candled, many-tongued
  Anticipation buoys her there.

Her beauty is her own spotlight:
  As she descends the talking dies;
And crystal lustres shine no more
  Than tears that start in ladies' eyes.

Her face is lit with holy joy,
  Her body moves in ice and flame;
He who looks into her eyes
  Can understand the Trojan shame.

The hubbub of the strings subsides;
  And now the final drums proclaim
The solo violin which sings
  The union of ice and flame.

Courageous tune that like a girl
  Can the listening crowd compel —
Perfection alone like this divides
  The human soul from death and hell.

Wolfgang Mozart's violin
  Leads me to the living stream;
There if I drink, the black abyss
  Is no more than a troubling dream.

JAMES REEVES

Stravinsky

He mounted the rostrum
Arms and coat-tails dangling.

The elegant ogre
Raised his wand.

The violins plucked
Nervously.

With quick strokes
He lashed the orchestra.

The oboe made
Fugitive sounds.

And the brass gave
Loud yelps.

JULIAN COOPER

To the Gentleman in Row D

Dear Sir, we in Row D are well aware
Your soul is steeped in music to the core.
You love, we notice, each succeeding air
More deeply than the one which came before.

You lead the orchestra in perfect time,
With ever-nodding head you set the pace,
We in Row D consider it a crime
You are not in Sir Thomas Beecham's place.

Your lily hands most delicately haver,
Each phrase is ended with a graceful twist,
You know, it seems, each breve and semi-quaver,
And play them gently on your other wrist.

Sometimes you hum the least familiar portions,
And beat upon the floor a faint tattoo,
Though we can stand a lot of your contortions,
We shouldn't tap too much if we were you!

Dear Sir, we need no musical instructor,
We also sang in oratorio,
And if you were a really good conductor,
Our lightning would have struck you hours ago!

VIRGINIA GRAHAM

IN QUIRES AND PLACES WHERE THEY SING: CHURCH MUSIC

Church-Musick

Sweetest of sweets, I thank you: when displeasure
　　Did through my bodie wound my minde,
You took me thence, and in your house of pleasure
　　A daintie lodging me assign'd.

Now I in you without a bodie move,
　　Rising and falling with your wings:
We both together sweetly live and love,
　　Yet say sometimes, *God help poore Kings.*

Comfort, I'le die; for if you poste from me,
　　Sure I shall do so, and much more:
But if I travell in your companie,
　　You know the way to heaven's doore.

GEORGE HERBERT

King's College Chapel

When to the music of Byrd or Tallis,
　　The ruffed boys singing in the blackened stalls,
The candles lighting the small bones on their faces,
　　The Tudors stiff in marble on the walls,

There comes to evensong Elizabeth or Henry,
　　Rich with brocade, pearl, golden lilies, at the altar,
The scarlet lions leaping on their bosoms,
　　Pale royal hands fingering the crackling psalter,

Henry is thinking of his lute and of backgammon,
    Elizabeth follows the waving song, the mystery,
Proud in her red wig and green jewelled favours;
    They sit in their white lawn sleeves, as cool as history.

CHARLES CAUSLEY

Master Hugues of Saxe-Gotha

(an Unknown Musician)

Hist, but a word, fair and soft!
    Forth and be judged, Master Hugues!
Answer the question I've put you so oft —
    What do you mean by your mountainous fugues?
See, we're alone in the loft, —

I, the poor organist here,
    Hugues, the composer of note —
Dead, though, and done with, this many a year:
    Let's have a colloquy, something to quote,
Make the world prick up its ear!

See, the church empties apace:
    Fast they extinguish the lights —
Hallo there, sacristan! five minutes' grace!
    Here's a crank pedal wants setting to rights,
Baulks one of holding the base.

See, our huge house of the sounds,
    Hushing its hundreds at once,
Bids the last loiterer back to his bounds!
    — Oh, you may challenge them, not a response
Get the church-saints on their rounds!

(Saints go their rounds, who shall doubt?
   — March, with the moon to admire,
Up nave, down chancel, turn transept about,
   Supervise all betwixt pavement and spire,
Put rats and mice to the rout —

Aloys and Jurien and Just —
   Order things back to their place,
Have a sharp eye lest the candlesticks rust,
   Rub the church-plate, darn the sacrament-lace,
Clear the desk-velvet of dust.)

Here's your book, younger folks shelve!
   Played I not off-hand and runningly.
Just now, your masterpiece, hard number twelve?
   Here's what should strike, — could one handle it cunningly:
Help the axe, give it a helve!

Page after page as I played,
   Every bar's rest, where one wipes
Sweat from one's brow, I looked up and surveyed,
   O'er my three claviers, yon forest of pipes
Whence you still peeped in the shade.

Sure, you were wishful to speak,
   You, with brow ruled like a score,
Yes, and eyes buried in pits on each cheek,
   Like two great breves as they wrote them of yore
Each side that bar, your straight beak!

Sure you said — 'Good, the mere notes!
   Still, couldst thou take my intent,
Know what procured me our Company's votes —
   Masters being lauded and sciolists shent,
Parted the sheep from the goats!'

Well then, speak up, never flinch!
　　Quick, ere my candle's a snuff
— Burnt, do you see? to its uttermost inch —
　　I believe in you, but that's not enough:
Give my conviction a clinch!

First you deliver your phrase
　　— Nothing propound, that I see,
Fit in itself for much blame or much praise —
　　Answered no less, where no answer needs be:
Off start the Two on their ways!

Straight must a Third interpose,
　　Volunteer needlessly help —
In strikes a Fourth, a Fifth thrusts in his nose,
　　So the cry's open, the kennel's a-yelp,
Argument's hot to the close!

One dissertates, — he is candid;
　　Two must discept, — has distinguished!
Three helps the couple, if ever yet man did;
　　Four protests; Five makes a dart at the thing wished:
Back to One, goes the case bandied!

One says his say with a difference —
　　More of expounding, explaining!
All now is wrangle, abuse and vociferance —
　　Now there's a truce, all's subdued, self-restraining —
Five, though, stands out all the stiffer hence.

One is incisive, corrosive;
　　Two retorts, nettled, curt, crepitant;
Three makes rejoinder, expansive, explosive;
　　Four overbears them all, strident and strepitant:
Five . . . O Danaides, O Sieve!

Now, they ply axes and crowbars;
  Now, they prick pins at a tissue
Fine as a skein of the casuist Escobar's
  Worked on the bone of a lie. To what issue?
Where is our gain at the Two-bars?

Est fuga, volvitur rota!
  On we drift. Where looms the dim port?
One, Two, Three, Four, Five contribute their quota —
  Something is gained, if one caught but the import —
Show it us, Hugues of Saxe-Gotha!

What with affirming, denying,
  Holding, risposting, subjoining,
All's like . . . it's like . . . for an instance I'm trying . . .
  There! See our roof, its gilt moulding and groining
Under those spider-webs lying!

So your fugue broadens and thickens,
  Greatens and deepens and lengthens,
Till one exclaims — 'But where's music, the dickens?
  Blot ye the gold, while your spider-web strengthens
— Blacked to the stoutest of tickens?'

I for man's effort am zealous:
  Prove me such censure's unfounded!
Seems it surprising a lover grows jealous —
  Hopes 'twas for something his organpipes sounded,
Tiring three boys at the bellows?

Is it your moral of Life?
  Such a web, simple and subtle,
Weave we on earth here in impotent strife,
  Backward and forward each throwing his shuttle,
Death ending all with a knife?

Over our heads Truth and Nature —
　　Still our life's zigzags and dodges,
Ins and outs, weaving a new legislature —
　　God's gold just shining its last where that lodges,
Palled beneath Man's usurpature!

So we o'ershroud stars and roses,
　　Cherub and trophy and garland.
Nothing grow something which quietly closes
　　Heaven's earnest eye, — not a glimpse of the far land
Gets through our comments and glozes.

Ah, but traditions, inventions,
　　(Say we and make up a visage)
So many men with such various intentions
　　Down the past ages must know more than this age!
Leave the web all its dimensions!

Who thinks Hugues wrote for the deaf,
　　Proved a mere mountain in labour?
Better submit — try again — what's the clef?
　　'Faith, it's no trifle for pipe and for tabor —
Four flats, the minor in F.

Friend, your fugue taxes the finger:
　　Learning it once, who would lose it?
Yet all the while a misgiving will linger,
　　Truth's golden o'er us although we refuse it —
Nature, thro' dust-clouds we fling her!

Hugues! I advise *meâ poenâ*
　　(Counterpoint glares like a Gorgon)
Bid One, Two, Three, Four, Five, clear the arena!
　　Say the word, straight I unstop the Full-Organ,
Blare out the *mode Palestrina*.

While in the roof, if I'm right there,
    . . . Lo, you, the wick in the socket!
Hallo, you sacristan, show us a light there!
    Down it dips, gone like a rocket!
What, you want, do you, to come unawares,
Sweeping the church up for first morning-prayers,
And find a poor devil has ended his cares
At the foot of your rotten-runged rat-riddled stairs?
    Do I carry the moon in my pocket?

ROBERT BROWNING

The Choirmaster's Burial

He often would ask us
That, when he died,
After playing so many
To their last rest,
If out of us any
Should here abide,
And it would not task us,
We would with our lutes
Play over him
By his grave-brim
The psalm he liked best —
The one whose sense suits
'Mount Ephraim' —
And perhaps we should seem
To him, in Death's dream,
Like the seraphim.

As soon as I knew
That his spirit was gone
I thought this his due,
And spoke thereupon.
'I think', said the vicar,
'A read service quicker
Than viols out-of-doors
In these frosts and hoars.
That old-fashioned way
Requires a fine day,
And it seems to me
It had better not be.'

Hence, that afternoon,
Though never knew he
That his wish could not be,
To get through it faster
They buried the master
Without any tune.

But 'twas said that, when
At the dead of next night
The vicar looked out,
There struck on his ken
Thronged roundabout,
Where the frost was graying
The headstoned grass,
A band all in white
Like the saints in church-glass,
Singing and playing
The ancient stave
By the choirmaster's grave.

Such the tenor man told
When he had grown old.

THOMAS HARDY

Listening to Handel's 'Messiah'

Comfort ye, my people —
your face speaks out of the orchestra,
your hair entwined among the strings of violins,
the voice of the fugue,
the magnificent certainties of Handel:
And the glory of the Lord shall be revealed.
Lent and the primroses of childhood
in Pentewan Valley and the fields of Pondhu.
Behold He shall come, saith the Lord of Hosts.
But who may abide the day of His coming?
The pathos of life, the tenderness,
the infinite regret of the world,
the propitiation for mankind,
the garlands of women's voices singing *Hosanna,*
the comfort and strength of the men.
Emmanuel, Emmanuel, Emmanuel.
O thou that tellest good tidings to Zion.
The cities of Judah, Behold your God:
the afternoon sunlight,
the beams streaming in upon upturned faces,
here a young man in uniform,
there a girl's innocent face, hair under a ribbon,
the tides of music running through the veins,
uniting the people,
The people that walkèd in darkness
Have seen a great light.
Church bells, the church bells of Georgian England
Ring out in the inner world of the ear,
Sing in the heart,
The heart alone in all the throng of people.
For unto us a Child is born —
Alas, not unto us:
through the mist of sunlight music faces faith

I see your eyes following me,
I feel your presence.
My mind tells me
All the same this is an end:
the Thames at Abingdon,
the river bank at Easter, hawthorn in flower,
white sails on the blue river,
the reeds the wind the sun
a pastoral interlude, all at an end;
or walking the valley of the Windrush,
the cowslip-sweet banks by Minster Lovell,
the ruined manor across the water-meadows,
the clink of harness at the ford,
lingering with the music on the bridge,
looking into the still water and finding love,
while time stood still.
*There were shepherds abiding in the fields, keeping watch over their
    flocks*
And lo! the Angel of the Lord came upon them:
Glory to God, Glory to God, Glory to God in the highest.
The eyes filled with tears for the vanity of human hopes,
the music swirls round me
and I am lost,
lost in the contemplation of your absent heart
(where you are, how happy you make those).
The lovely fluted voice sings
How beautiful are the feet of them that preach the gospel of peace.
Does no echo reach you
where you tread the lanes of Kent,
rise in the moondawn to steal through the woods,
mount the hills, pack on back,
march all day hauling your beloved guns
till sundown and quiet evening,
bugles and comradeship and sleep?
Why do the nations so furiously rage together?
And why do the people imagine a vain thing?

Yet your golden nature complains not and is content.
I am left to realise in the music,
in the crowded hall, in others' happiness,
that all the same this is an end.

A. L. ROWSE

Delius in the Cathedral

Trees crept into church,
Stood nave-high against pillars
Wearing flutes in their branches.
Hemmed softly with strings
They weaved rafters, clefs, and in the aisles
God knelt to listen. Faces grew
Out of the pillar trunks
Pierced by swords moving in motes
Lit rose window wise; fields lay;
Altar, trout-stream over, bridged
Delius through the green choir-stalls.
I sat under a stone arras — was not sure
It was not oak; listened verdantly,
While hares came out under my seat
And clustered, waiting for the corn.

DEREK PARKER

Choirs

Does memory make you sad of heart?
   No, I'll not trust those ancient tales,
Though you should make my tears to start,
   You choirs of soulless nightingales:

For I've heard twenty rogues today,
   Your rivals, flouting gods and men,
Come laughing into Church from play,
   Rustle their surplices, and then

To heavens higher than all height
   From rascal throats unfaltering raise
A Jacob's ladder of pure light,
   A single sanctity of praise.

GEORGE ROSTREVOR HAMILTON

The Hymn Tunes

They often haunt me, these substantial ghosts,
Four-four, four-square, thumping in the brain;
Not always with the words their puritan
Plainness was made to, and yet always plain,
Bawdily forthright, loud for Lord of Hosts.
One must begin somewhere.
        Where I began

I sang off-key on Low Church, tropical
Sunday mornings; organ-swept, never doubted
That the sure tunes had reason to be sure,
That some great good would come of what I shouted.
Later, across the sea, I sang in a tall
Gothic cathedral, where all sounds endure

Long seconds in the vault, but felt no change
In what the tunes were. And when, later still,
I learned new smut to sing to the old notes,
They stayed the same. Nothing changed until
I woke one day to find the rules were strange
I'd thought to obey.
        Now a hymn-tune floats

Teasingly into the mind, patterns a day
To its rhythm, and nags like sudden speech
In a tongue one used to know — quietly said
Words which never move forward, always out of reach;
Still, though I cannot grasp what it is they say,
God's tunes go marching through my echoing head.

EDWARD LUCIE-SMITH

Singing Children: Luca Della Robbia (T.H.)

I see you, angels with choirboy faces,
  Trilling it from the museum wall
As once, decani or cantoris,
  You sang in a carved oak stall,
Nor deemed any final bar to such time-honoured carollings
  E'er could befall.

I too gave tongue in my piping youth-days,
  Yea, took like a bird to crotchet and clef,
Antheming out with a will the Old Hundredth,
  Salem, or Bunnett in F,
Unreckoning even as you if the Primal Sapience
  Be deaf, stone-deaf.

Many a matins cheerfully droned I
  To the harmonium's clacking wheeze,
Fidgeted much through prayer and sermon
  While errant bumblebees
Drummed on the ivied window, veering my thoughts to
  Alfresco glees.

But voices break — aye, and more than voices;
  The heart for hymn tune and haytime goes.
Dear Duomo choristers, chirping for ever
  In jaunty, angelic pose,
Would I had sung my last ere joy-throbs dwindled
  Or wan faith froze!

C. DAY LEWIS

Seated One Day

'The Syrinx of olden times, which was to become the *frestel* of the minstrels, is still used in the Balkans and by the goatherds of the Pyrenees, who burble limpid tunes by blowing into their *piharets* or *pihurlecs* . . . the organ also includes reed-stops; their ancestors may be found in the Greek *aulos* . . . as also in the Chinese *cheng* or mouth-organ . . . the Romans used them, as is evident from the *tibia utricularis*. From this instrument originated the Breton *cornemuse*, or *biniou*, the *cabrette* of Auvergne, the Italian *zampogna*, the Spanish and Portuguese *gaita*, the Scottish *bagpipes*, etc.' — *Organ Music*, Leduc.

Up in his loft the shy FRCO
Pours splendour on the shufflers–out below
Whose thoughts now run more on the Sunday joint
Than mounting majesties of counterpoint
And only six or seven, whose souls are finer,
Stay for the climax of the great G Minor
Or for the player's public-private dream
(Since Improvising On A Given Theme
Was one of many subjects passed in, all
In that odd building near the Albert Hall).
O, what musician stands comparison
With maestros of the Willis or the Harrison
And Harrison? O artists in the round
Rearing colossal palaces of sound
Or, if a dreamy air be thought the best,
Drawing sweet sadness from the *Voix Céleste!*
Here in my verse your ancestry I blazon,
Ye ancient heroes of the diapason.

Long before Europe knows of loud-voic'd choirs
The goat-foot God with *syrinx*-note inspires
And Balkan shepherds burble limpid tunes
First played by Fauns on far-off Afternoons;

Bach wrote some down — not all; the rest'll
Only be heard on *piharet* or *frestel*
Only where Bretons guard their lambs and ewes
Is heard the full magic of the *cornemuse*.
See how the organ owes an ancient debt
To the wild *bagpipes* and the loud *cabrette*,
See, where the southern light grows ever brighter
The Portuguese wakes echoes with his *gaita*
Which, like the *cheng* amid the paddy crops,
Sounds even reedier than French organ stops.
For *cheng* and *aulos*, *biniou* and *flute*
All issue forth from music's ancient root;
Now your great engine keeps them all in station;
Here, at the fount of music's console-ation
By art the wild notes now are organised,
By art the song of Pan is christianised:
  Hail to you, organists, who, behind a screen
  Each day reveal the God in the Machine.

PAUL JENNINGS

The Lost Chord

Seated one day at the organ
  I jumped as if I'd been shot,
For the Dean was upon me, snarling
  'Stainer — and *make it hot*'.

All week I swung Stainer and Barnby,
  Bach, Gounod, and Bunnett in A;
I said, 'Gosh, the old bus is a wonder!'
  The Dean, with a nod, said 'Okay'.

D. B. WYNDHAM LEWIS

OPERA NIGHTS

Grand Opera

The lovers have poisoned themselves and died singing,
And the crushed peasant father howls in vain.
For his duplicity, lubricity and greed
The unspeakable base count is horribly slain.

After the music, after the applause,
The lights go up, the final curtain drops.
The clerks troop from the house, and some are thinking:
Why is life different when the singing stops?

All that hysteria and those histrionics,
All those coincidences were absurd.
But if there were no relevance to life,
Why were they moved to shudder and applaud?

Though they outlived their passion, it was theirs,
As was the jealousy, the sense of wrong
When some proud jack-in-office trampled them;
Only it did not goad them into song.

The accidents, the gross misunderstandings,
Paternal sorrow, amorous frustration
Have they not suffered? Was the melodrama
An altogether baseless imitation?

JAMES REEVES

A Performance of 'Boris Godunov'

The fur-cloaked boyars plotting in the hall,
The heavy splendours of the palace room,
The monk intoning litanies from old
Parchment in the great cell's timeless gloom,
Keep tense beneath the Russian music's weight,
Demoniac or numinous with doom.

Even the False Demetrius is caught;
The silver armour, dark-eyed paler face,
The Polish gardens and romantic love:
There is no weight or depth in all that grace.
Only the Jesuits are black and cold
— He knows them shallow, knows his doom and place.

Down in the church, vibrations scarcely heard
Beneath the senses tolls the slow, huge bell.
The silent, smoking candles give their gleam
To themes on which the holy paintings dwell
With artlessness that comes of certainty
— The terrifying crudities of Hell.

Even the drunken friars, the peasant dance,
The claimant's quick ambition, are a froth
On depths that pour into the dark Tsar's heart
Unlit by white Ionian or red Goth,
Where Athos, Sinai and the Thebaid
Glide darkly from Time's vaults, past secret Thoth.

But that dark river is the music now:
Not hope nor love nor thought can will it dry;
The priests and boyars stand round like a wall,
And as the anthems sweep him off to die
The drowning Tsar hears dimly through their voice
The hallucination of eternity.

ROBERT CONQUEST

French Horns

Kaff. 1943

A Benefit Night at the Opera

The chatter thins, lights dip, and dusty crimson
Curtains start dragging away. Then, at one bound,
A rush of trumpets, ringing brass and vermilion —
The frescoed nymphs sprawl in a sea of sound.

We give our best attention as we must, for
This music is fatal and must be heard.
The glittering fountains vocalize our lust,
The whole brilliant scene sways on to murder.

The idyll interrupted by a cough,
Coloratura soars into a fever.
After the vows, the sibyl shuffles off,
The conspirators' chorus mutter, melt away, leave us

A traitor and his stabbed tyrant, downstage in tears.
Masked revellers are grouping for a wedding.
In stern beat start to life six scarlet halberdiers,
Move with the music, march to a beheading.

Lo! Wild applause proclaims a happy ending.
Vendetta is achieved with clinking swords.
Sheer from the battlements the Diva is descending,
Rash in black velvet and resplendent chords.

MARTIN BELL

Dunces' Opera

When lo! a harlot form[1] soft sliding by,
With mincing step, small voice, and languid eye:
Foreign her air, her robe's discordant pride
In patch-work flutt'ring, and her head aside:
By singing peers upheld on either hand,
She tripped and laughed, too pretty much to stand;
Cast on the prostrate Nine a scornful look,
Then thus in quaint recitativo spoke.

'O Cara! Cara! silence all that train:
Joy to great Chaos! let division reign:[2]
Chromatic tortures soon shall drive them hence,
Break all their nerves and fritter all their sense:
One trill shall harmonise joy, grief, and rage,
Wake the dull church, and lull the ranting stage;
To the same notes thy sons shall hum, or snore,
And all thy yawning daughters cry, "Encore".
Another Phoebus, thy own Phoebus, reigns,
Joys in my jigs, and dances in my chains.
But soon, ah soon, rebellion will commence,
If music meanly borrows aid from sense.

[1] 'The attitude given to this phantom represents the nature and genius
of the Italian opera; its affected airs, its effeminate sounds, and the
practice of patching up these operas with favourite songs, incoherently
put together. These things were supported by the subscriptions of the
nobility.'—POPE.
[2] 'Alluding to the false taste of playing tricks in music with numberless
divisions, to the neglect of that harmony which conforms to the sense and
applies to the passions. Mr Handel had introduced a great number of
hands and more variety of instruments into the orchestra, and employed
even drums and cannon to make a fuller chorus; which proved so much
too manly for the fine gentlemen of his age, that he was obliged to
remove his music into Ireland. After which they were reduced, for want of
composers, to practise the patch-work above-mentioned.'—POPE.

Strong in new arms, lo! Giant Handel stands,
Like bold Briareus, with a hundred hands;
To stir, to rouse, to shake the soul he comes,
And Jove's own thunders follow Mars's Drums.
Arrest him, empress; or you sleep no more — '
She heard, and drove him to the Hibernian shore.

ALEXANDER POPE: from *The Dunciad, Book IV*

After the Opera

Down the stone stairs
Girls with their large eyes wide with tragedy
Lift looks of shocked and momentous emotion up at me.
And I smile.

Ladies
Stepping like birds with their bright and pointed feet
Peer anxiously forth, as if for a boat to carry them out of the
    wreckage;
And among the wreck of the theatre crowd
I stand and smile.
They take tragedy so becomingly;
Which pleases me.

But when I meet the weary eyes
The reddening, aching eyes of the bar-man with thin arms,
I am glad to go back to where I came from.

D. H. LAWRENCE

Verdi at Eighty

My brides are ravished away, are ravished away,
Two Leonoras, Gilda, Violetta,
One swaggering tenor has taken them,
One death seduced them to fever.

I have contrived a basso politics
To hunt him down, conspired
Through trio and quartette, strong situations,
Needled him on to my avenging sword.

2

How shall a wicked, fat, old man be saved?
Connive with the women, incessant giggles and whispers.
He must be re-baptised in muddy water
And wash the district's dirty linen with him.
The wine will chirrup, an insect in old veins.
Ready then assume the sacrificial horns,
Grovel in terror before the Fairy Queen,
So that, our hope, lost lovers may re-join:
Nanetta find a tenor in the woods.
The festival will glow in basso nimbus of laughter.

MARTIN BELL

THE INSTRUMENTS
OF JOY

The Lekingfelde Proverbs

The Harpe is an instrumente of swete molodye,
Rude intelligens of the sounde conceyvethe no armonye;
But who so in that instrumente hathe no speculacion,
What restithe withyn the sounde borde hathe but smale
   probacion.

He that is a perfyte musicion
Perceyvithe the Lute tewnes and the goode proporcion;
In myddest of the body the stringis sowndith best,
For, stoppide in the freytis, they abyde the pynnes wrest.

A slac strynge in a Virgynall soundithe not aright;
It dothe abyde no wrastinge, it is so louse and light.
The sounde borde crasede forsith the instrumente
Throw mysgovernaunce to make notis whiche was not his intent.

The Recorder of his kynde the meane dothe desyre;
Manyfolde fyngerynge and stoppes bryngithe hym from his tunes
   clere:
Who so lyst to handill an instrumente so goode
Must se in his many fyngerynge that he kepe tyme, stop and
   moode.

A Shawme makithe a swete sounde, for he tunythe basse;
It mountithe not to hy, but kepithe rule and space.
Yet yf it be blown withe to a vehement wynde,
It makithe it to mysgoverne oute of his kynde.

Immoderate wyndes in a Clarion causithe it for to rage;
Soft wynde and moderate makithe the sounde to assuage.
Therfore he whiche in that instrument wolde have swete
   modulacion,
Bustius wyndes must leve and use moderacion.

The swete Orgayne pipis comfortith a stedfast mynde;
Wronge handlynge of the stoppis may cause them sypher from
  their kynde.
But he that playethe of pipis, wher so grete nowmber is,
Must handill the keyes all lyke that (by) mysgovernaunce they
  sownde (not) amysse.

The modulacion of Musyke is swete and celestiall,
In the spheris of the planettis makynge sownde armonicall;
If we moder oure Musyke as the trewe tune is,
In hevyn we shall synge OSANNA IN EXCELSIS.

ANON., sixteenth century

English Musical Instruments

Of sundry sorts that were, as the musician likes,
On which the practis'd hand with perfect fingering strikes,
Whereby their height of skill might liveliest be exprest.
The trembling lute some touch, some strain the viol best
In sets which there were seen, the music wondrous choice.
Some likewise there affect the gamba[1] with the voice,
To show that England could variety afford.
Some that delight to touch the sterner wiry chord
The cittern, the pandore,[2] and the theorbo[3] strike;
The gittern[4] and the kit[5] the wand'ring fiddles like.
So were there some again, in this their learned strife,
Loud instruments that loved; the cornet and the fife,
The hautboy[6], sackbut[7] deep, recorder and the flute,
Even from the shrillest shawm[8] on to the cornamute[9].
Some blow the bagpipe up that plays the country round,
The tabor and the pipe some take delight to sound.

MICHAEL DRAYTON from Polyolbion

[1] viol held between the legs   [2] plucked string instrument of lute type
[3] large lute   [4] guitar   [5] small type of violin, played by dancing masters
[6] oboe   [7] trombone   [8] forerunner of oboe   [9] form of bagpipe

Marie Liska
— an interruption

Katt '48

A Song for St Cecilia's Day, November 22, 1687

From Harmony, from heav'nly Harmony
    This universal Frame began;
  When Nature underneath a heap
    Of jarring Atomes lay,
  And cou'd not heave her Head,
The tuneful Voice was heard from high,
    Arise, ye more than dead.
Then cold and hot and moist and dry
  In order to their Stations leap,
    And MUSICK'S pow'r obey.
From Harmony, from heavenly Harmony
    This universal Frame began:
    From Harmony to Harmony
Through all the Compass of the Notes it ran,
The Diapason closing full in Man.

What Passion cannot MUSICK raise and quell?
    When *Jubal* struck the corded Shell,
  His listening Brethren stood around,
    And, wond'ring, on their Faces fell
  To worship that Celestial Sound:
Less than a God they thought there could not dwell
    Within the hollow of that Shell,
    That spoke so sweetly, and so well.
What Passion cannot MUSICK raise and quell?

    The TRUMPET'S loud Clangor
      Excites us to Arms
    With shrill Notes of Anger
      And mortal Alarms.
    The double double double beat
      Of the thund'ring DRUM
      Cryes, heark the Foes come;
Charge, Charge, 'tis too late to retreat.

The soft complaining FLUTE
In dying Notes discovers
The Woes of hopeless Lovers,
Whose Dirge is whisper'd by the warbling LUTE.
Sharp VIOLINS proclaim
Their jealous Pangs and Desperation,
Fury, frantick Indignation,
Depth of Pains and Height of Passion,
For the fair, disdainful Dame.

But oh! what Art can teach
What human Voice can reach
The sacred ORGAN'S Praise?
Notes inspiring holy Love,
Notes that wing their heavenly Ways
To mend the Choires above.

Orpheus cou'd lead the savage race,
And Trees unrooted left their Place,
Sequacious of the Lyre;
But bright CECILIA rais'd the Wonder high'r:
When to her Organ vocal Breath was given,
An Angel heard, and straight appear'd
Mistaking Earth for Heav'n.

GRAND CHORUS

As from the Pow'r of Sacred Lays
The Spheres began to move,
And sung the great Creator's Praise
To all the bless'd above;
So, when the last and dreadful Hour
This crumbling Pageant shall devour,
The TRUMPET shall be heard on high,
The dead shall live, the living die,
And MUSICK shall untune the Sky.

JOHN DRYDEN

Instrument Rhimes

For H is a spirit and therefore he is God.
For K is king and therefore he is God.
For L is love and therefore he is God.
For M is musick and therefore he is God.
For the instruments are by their rhimes
For the Shawm rhimes are lawn fawn moon boom and the like
For the harp rhimes are sing ring string and the like
For the cymbal rhimes are bell well toll soul and the like
For the flute rhimes are tooth youth suit mute and the like
For the Bassoon rhimes are pass class and the like
For the dulcimer rhimes are grace place beat heat and the like
For the Clarinet rhimes are clean seen and the like
For the trumpet rhimes are sound bound soar more and the like.
For the TRUMPET of God is a blessed intelligence and so are
   all the instruments in HEAV'N.
For God the father Almighty plays upon the HARP of stupendous
   magnitude and melody.
For at that time malignity ceases and the devils themselves are at
   peace.
For this time is perceptible to man by a remarkable stillness and
   serenity of soul.
Hallelujah from the heart of God, and from the hand of the
   artist inimitable, and from the echo of the heavenly harp in
   sweetness magnifical and mighty.

CHRISTOPHER SMART from *Jubilate Agno*

Musick Commended, and Scraping Ridiculed, etc.

I

Since *Musick* so delights the Sense,
   And charms each Lover's Breast,
Let us, of all the Instruments,
   Try which will please the best.
Hark how the chearful Violin
   Its Silver Sounds sends forth,
Whose sprightly Notes our Hearts incline
   To Musick and to Mirth.
As the wandering Planets,
   Who never are idle,
The Musical Spheres
   In their Motions obey;
Ev'n so does my Soul
   At the Sound of a Fiddle
Dance merrily round
   Its inclosure of Clay.
Or when it breathes its softer Airs,
   So melting, so Divinely sweet,
I could dissolve in Tears and Pray'rs
   At charming *Chloe's* Feet.
But when a bold Hand,
   With a Grace like a *Bacchus*,
Most manfully Thrashes
   The Strings 'till they rattle;
No Beautiful Nymph
   With her Charms dare attack us;
The Punk we defy,
   And incline to the Bottle.

II

Hark how the Organ next commands
   Our Ears with awful Pow'r;

No singing Swans in softer Strains
　　Foretel their dying Hour.
To Heav'n it elevates the Mind,
　　And with Devotion fills the Heart;
No Nightingails in Consort joyn'd
　　Can sweeter Harmony impart.
But when it is touch'd
　　At the *Star* or the *Gun*,
By some blind begging Bag-piper's
　　Son for a Devil,
Who does with one Hand
　　Vamp a Base to a Tune,
Whilst the other is wiping
　　His Nose from the Snivel;
O! what Musick it yields,
　　With a tone like a Drum
That would make a Man sick
　　Tho' admir'd by some:
Whilst Soldiers and Sea-men,
　　Boys, Wenches, and Women,
Some dancing like Bears,
　　Others lending their Ears
To the Doodle and Squeak,
　　Toot a Toot, and a Hum.

III

The Viol's in the Master's Hand;
　　The Lyre-Way Tunes he plays
Your Grave Attention will command,
　　Whilst with its charming Lays
He does each list'ning Soul delight,
And with his Cadences invite
　　Our Tongues to sing his Praise.
　　　But when pretty Miss
　　　Sidles upon her Knees,
And slips in the Viol between 'em!

How she scrapes and she sings,
And bedevils the Strings,
As if nothing but Discord were in 'em!
With her Trills and her Shakes
Such a Howling she makes
That a Consort of Cats
From her Musick would run.
With a Finger on a Fret;
Zingle, zingle, zingle, whet,
When a Squeak up in Alt,
Here a Fault, then a Halt,
So my Lady has done.

IV

Now, listen to the am'rous Flute,
You loving Nymphs and Swains;
'Twould make sweet *Philomel* turn Mute
To hear its softer Strains.
What warbling Notes delight the Ear:
What pleasure do we find!
What sordid Anch'rite could forbear
The Thoughts of Love, were he to hear
Musick so charming and so kind?
But when City Beau,
Powder'd up for a Show,
Sits behind his Counter a Piping,
With his Musick-Book spread,
Beating Time with his Head,
It would give Man's Guts the Griping.
The Tune that he loves
Is *O happy Groves*,
Which the Dunce so confoundedly touches,
'Till he slabbers his Pipe.
Then he gives it a wipe,
And forbears when his Master approaches.

V

Hark how the Trumpet's Warlike Tone
    Tantara rara sounds to the Battel.
Who from its Marshal Voice could run,
    Or quit the Field tho' ne'er so fatal?
The bold Heroick Strains we hear,
Were they to reach a Dastard's Ear,
    Must sure inspire him to be Brave,
When such a Harmony is nigh.
Rather than like a Coward fly,
    Who would not chuse a Grave?
But when the Brazen Trumpet's held
    Aloft, a L—d M—r's Raree-show,
The Cheeks like Foot-balls first are swell'd,
    Then blow, Cuckolds, blow.
My L—d his Trumpets much commends,
    And vows they chear his Heart,
Tho' all this windy Musick ends
    In Fart, Fart, Fart.

Chorus

Come, Violins, again begin,
    Assisted with our Bases;
No Bungler here shall teaz the Ear
    With *Wapping* Slurs or Graces.
O Organ! let thy Heav'nly Sound
    Inspire us to perform.
In thee all Harmony is found
    That can the Fancy warm.
Come, Viol, soften with thy Notes
    The various Sounds we hear.
Assist us all, ye charming Flutes,
    To please the list'ning Ear.

That all may in a *Chorus* joyn,
   Sound the Trumpet, sound.
Since Musick is Divine,
   Let Harmony go round.

Grand Chorus

Our Songs and our Musick
   Let's still dedicate
To *Purcel*, to *Purcel*,
   The Son of *Apollo*,
'Till another, another,
   Another as Great
In the Heav'nly Science
   Of Musick shall follow.

THOMAS D'URFEY

The Mandoline

What fingers plucked these long untroubled strings?
Or, in their ambience, whose uprising voice
Soared into song on gently clamorous wings
Bidding the shy, Victorian heart rejoice?
Inlaid with lilies and a wreath of leaves,
Carved by some lad in Naples years ago —
Surely his restive spirit, loitering, grieves
That it should be at last discarded so,
Kicked in a corner, dusty, daubed with grime,
Unseen, untouched, untended, wholly dumb.
Only those ghosts who keep no count of time,
Brief in their nightly visitations, come
And like the easeful strumming of the rain
Waken its sentient chords to sound again.

JEAN KENWARD

The Violin

If there be soul in wood and strings
To humour thus the quiet night,
If matter dead so strives, and sings
Such glory, with such transitory,
Spontaneous, tremulous sounds attesting,
With cadences like rose leaves shed
When keen sweet winds disperse delight,
Radiance revealing, rising, resting,
Declining, drooping, dying, dead.

Impetuous to rise again
Like fire, like wild fire's flaming flakes,
Like high-hurled spray on moon-lit main,
Like a fountain throwing liquid light,
Bearing such joy to such a height,
Scattering delight in such swift shakes,
Lending desire such subtle wings —
All this the simple wood and strings
With human hand to guide it, makes.

What sounds should I, so complex more,
Constructed with such artifice,
So full of wonder and device,
Surrounded with such happy store
Of miracle to celebrate,
New visions sprung with each new date,
Of fields unknown, and paths untrod,
What sounds should I then resonate
Beneath the urgent hand of God?

E. N. DA C. ANDRADE

Materia Musica

LEATHER

for

ORGANS, PIANO ACTIONS AND ALL WIND
INSTRUMENTS
BELLOWS, STRAINS, HALF-STRAINS, PALLETS,
GUSSETS, BEDDING, PNEUMATIC LAMBS,
BROWN AND WHITE PNEUMATIC SPLITS,
SUMAC SKIVERS, ZEPHYR AND SIMILI SKINS
— advert in *Musical Opinion*

Marvellous music laps me round
Dissolving my soul in a sea of sound;
Down in the sea where I am drowned
The dark is I and I am the dark
Where light created shines pure and stark,
Where I am the sea and I am the ark;
The shapes of light and of dark in me
Swell to the bounds of that primal sea
Where to be dissolved is the more to *be* —

The words are wild, and I cannot say,
Back in the common unmusical day
Where in the world the reality lay —
Composer's mind where it all took root,
Giving this to the fiddle and that to the flute?
Players? Conductor? *Me*, though mute?

But odd that so many immortal airs
Depend upon leather, like shoe repairs
And STRAINS (or HALF-STRAINS, half-ethereal)
Need this pedestrian raw material.
In vain the composers have lived their lives
Unless in some attic the skiver skives
With SUMAC SKIVER (and skiving mallet?)

Fashioning GUSSET and BEDDING and PALLET
Attached with linkages, levers and cams
To PNEUMATIC, mysterious, musical LAMBS.
Hear the great soloist phrase with feeling —
But first came this glorified soling-and-heeling.
Many a glorious sound begins
With the sorting of ZEPHYR and SIMILI SKINS,
And never a valve in a horn or a trumpet
But skiver must skive it and mallet must thump it,
And many cadenzas and showing-off bits
Test BROWN (or WHITE) PNEUMATIC SPLITS. . . .

Marvellous music, that takes by storm
With changing vision of changeless Form
Here is your hidden divinity spied —
In a mystical game of seek-and-HIDE.

PAUL JENNINGS

Sandalwood Song

Sweet clavichord
Of whom the keys are ribs
And your body its casket
Made of sandalwood

Magical instrument now with open lid
Waiting, lying still,
For fingers to touch the notes . . .

SACHEVERELL SITWELL

A Lover of Music to his Pianoforte

Oh friend, whom glad or grave we seek,
   Heaven holding shrine!
I ope thee, touch thee, hear thee speak,
   And peace is mine.
No fairy casket full of bliss
   Out-values thee:
Love only, wakened with a kiss,
   More sweet may be.

To thee, when our full hearts o'erflow
   In grief or joys,
Unspeakable emotions owe
   A flitting voice:
Mirth flies to thee, and love's unrest,
   And Memory dear,
And Sorrow, with his tightening breast,
   Comes for a tear.

Oh since few joys of human mould
   Thus wait us still,
Twice blessed be thine, thou gentle fold
   Of peace at will.
No change, no sullenness, no cheat,
   In thee we find;
Thy saddest voice is ever sweet,
   Thine answer, kind.

LEIGH HUNT

COMPOSERS AND THEIR MUSIC

William Byrd

I have come very far, Lord. In my time
Men's mouths have been shut up, the gabble and whine
Of shot has drowned the singing. You will pardon
My praise that rises only from a book —
(How long shall that book be hidden
Under a scarecrow gown, under evil writings?)
And you will pardon the tricks, the secret rooms,
The boarded windows, your house against a stall.
These things have made my house of praise more holy.
And so I try to remember how it was
When lovers sang like finches, and the Word
Was music.
          Lord, I am no coward,
But an old man remembering the candle-flames
Reflected in the scroll-work, frozen trees
Praying for Advent, the willow cut at Easter.
The quires are dumb. My spirit sings in silence.
You will appoint the day of my arising.

SIDNEY KEYES

De Fesch[1]

For you I search my reference books in vain,
Willem of the impossible name De Fesch.
Vienna was it, Venice, or Amsterdam
Whose plain citizens knew you in the flesh?

Midnight has fallen; the wind unpacified
Moves in the outer darkness while I think
Of that odd sound: not grand, like Palestrina,
Nor quaint, like Dittersdorf or Humperdinck.

[1] sometimes written Defesch. This Belgian musician (1697–1758)
settled in London 1731—J.B.

Willem de Fesch would seem to be sound
Not shaped predestinately for high fame;
Nevertheless tonight it pleases me
To celebrate your spirit with your name.

By way of certain pieces for two 'cellos
That spirit earlier breathed upon the air.
Even in an age renowned for melody
Your phrase was of a quality so rare
It spoke out of no time to any time
When a dry heart might wither from despair.

JAMES REEVES

To My Friend Mr Henry Lawes

Harry, whose tuneful and well measur'd song
    First taught our English music how to span
    Words with just note and accent, not to scan
With Midas' ears, committing short and long;
Thy worth and skill exempts thee from the throng,
    With praise enough, for Envy to look wan;
    To after age thou shalt be writ the man,
That with smooth air couldst humour best our tongue.
Thou honour'st Verse, and Verse must send her wing,
    To honour thee, the priest of Phoebus' choir
        That tun'st their happiest lines in hymn, or story.
    Dante shall give Fame leave to set thee higher
Than his Casella, whom he wooed to sing
    Met in the milder shades of Purgatory.

JOHN MILTON

Mozart Recital at home   Kapp '62

Henry Purcell

The poet wishes well to the divine genius of Purcell and praises him
that, whereas other musicians have given utterance to the moods of man's
mind, he has, beyond that, uttered in notes the very make and species of
man as created both in him and in all men generally.

Have fair fallen, O fair, fair have fallen, so dear
To me, so arch-especial a spirit as heaves in Henry Purcell,
An age is now since passed, since parted; with the reversal
Of the outward sentence low lays him, listed to a heresy, here.

Not mood in him nor meaning, proud fire or sacred fear,
Or love, or pity, or all the sweet notes nor his might nursle:
It is the forgèd feature finds me; it is the rehearsal
Of own, of abrúpt sélf there so thrusts on, so throngs the ear.

Let him oh! with his air of angels then lift me, lay me! only I'll
Have an eye to the sakes of him, quaint moonmarks, to his pelted
    plummage under
Wings: so some great stormfowl, whenever he has walked his
    while

The thunder-purple seabeach, plumèd purple-of-thunder,
If a wuthering of his palmy snow-pinions scatter a colossal smile
Off him, but meaning motion fans fresh our wits with wonder.

GERARD MANLEY HOPKINS

On an Air of Rameau

To Arnold Dolmetsch

A melancholy desire of ancient things
Floats like a faded perfume out of the wires;
Pallid lovers, what unforgotten desires,
Whispered once, are retold in your whisperings?

Roses, roses, and lilies with hearts of gold,
These you plucked for her, these she wore in her breast;
Only Rameau's music remembers the rest,
The death of roses over a heart grown cold.

But these sighs? Can ghosts then sigh from the tomb?
Life then wept for you, sighed for you, chilled your breath?
It is the melancholy of ancient death
The harpsichord dreams of, sighing in the room.

ARTHUR SYMONS

A Sonata by Scarlatti

This music which you made, Domenico,
To smooth the boredom of a Queen of Spain —
Vivid as darting fireflies, sharp as Naples limes:
Now come the fifes and drums, the hunting-horns,
The bold announcing trumpets, and flambeaux carried
By black-sheathed, silk-eyed pages.
How brave, how gay that bright procession passes
Against the velvet night —
Against the crouching and carnivorous darkness!

JOHN HEATH-STUBBS

A Bach Cantata

How did he know our age,
Gnawn, bitter, riven?
Time like eroded stone
Or the bleak raven?

Around his bare notes
Voices of the living
Fit skins of air,
And the stones sing.

From a time of crystal
And the quiet city
The voice is speaking
In pity, in pity.

Listening, our hearts
Beat, echoing his own.
Chords linked, strong as hands
Make our kinship known.

MARGARET STANLEY-WRENCH

Homage to J. S. Bach

It is good just to think about Johann Sebastian
Bach, grinding away like the mills of God,
Producing masterpieces, and legitimate children —
Twenty-one in all — and earning his bread

Instructing choirboys to sing their *ut re mi*,
Provincial and obscure. When Fame's trumpets told
Of Handel displaying magnificent wings of melody,
Setting the waters of Thames on fire with gold,

Old Bach's music did not seem to the point:
He groped in the Gothic vaults of polyphony,
Labouring pedantic miracles of counterpoint.
They did not know that the order of eternity

Transfiguring the order of the Age of Reason,
The timeless accents of super-celestial harmonies,
Filtered into time through that stupendous brain.
It was the dancing angels in their hierarchies,

Teaching at the heart of Reason that Passion existed,
And at the heart of Passion a Crucifixion,
When the great waves of his *Sanctus* lifted
The blind art of music into a blinding vision.

JOHN HEATH-STUBBS

Mozart's 'Linz' Symphony

All is secure. The Hapsburg on his throne;
From silver sconces waxen candles cast
The only shadows, falling on damask walls,
Civilized music, disciplined, serene
Breathes from the oboe, from the muted horn,
And the remote fifes, like the threat of war,
Still leaving the heart untouched, and no one knows
That over green fields ten thousand march to die.

Yet in that soil the seeds we reap were sown,
Under the discipline spread that corrosion
That gnaws our conscience; derelict farm and village,
Sacked church and pillaged cloister, a country ravaged
By centuries of robbery and war.
Under its civilized disguise the heart
Breaking to know man's old misuse of man,
Speaks in the hollow voices of the horns,

And, in the flutes, children who cry and pull
At the skirt of a woman fretful and complaining;
Europe sickening, and Vienna starving,
And, a few years ahead, the pauper's grave.
Yet, for our comfort, in years that bring no comfort
The music, as brittle and silver as sunlight, wrung
From the still pause, the trembling brink of storms,
Holds a man's courage and immortality.

MARGARET STANLEY-WRENCH

Mozart

The sunshine, and the grace of falling rain,
The fluttering daffodil, the lilt of bees,
The blossom on the boughs of almond trees,
The waving of the wheat upon the plain —

And all that knows not effort, strife nor strain,
And all that bears the signature of ease,
The plunge of ships that dance before the breeze,
The flight across the twilight of the crane:

And all that joyous is, and young, and free,
That tastes of morning and the laughing surf;
The dawn, the dew, the newly turned-up turf,

The sudden smile, the unexpressive prayer,
The artless art, the untaught dignity; —
You speak them in the passage of an air.

MAURICE BARING

Mozart

Glacier song in the keen wind of April
I would construct you on this brink of air;
but fear to, so my flight must learn politeness
and dance in palaces where sorrow's rare.

Delighted with my melodies, yet wild,
I shall soar up to pinnacles that man
can climb and map with ease; only beyond
the bounds of joy my wonder longs to scan.

They call me angel, but I dread the fire
that shatters gracefulness and subtlety;
in the world's trouble I have been content
to weave a shape that sings serenity.

Do not forget, though, that I have not told
all that you need to know; down in the night
Beethoven roars, and far above my joy
Bach's mercy radiates your inmost sight.

Say this of me alone: I gave you fire
shaped to a brilliant essence in the heart,
giving it life; should you not want me now
I am content; in Hell I have no part.

CHARLES HIGHAM

Mozart at Zell-am-See

Who finds for Figaro's sake
Harmony sprung from storm?
Out of nothing the brain
Gathers unerring form
Over the Zeller lake,
And the miracle stirs again.

So may the ripples drift,
Playing their facile song.
As a salmon leaps to the fly
Out of the current, strong
Into its arc the gift
Ascends, and alters the sky.

Whether foolish or wise,
Cutting the course of time,
Music leaves the unknown.
Wherever delight would climb
In the light of a young girl's eyes
That light in the scales is shown.

How does Mozart transpose
What is unknown to man
Except in innocent joy?
This that from nothing ran
Leaps from its very close
To enchant the dreaming boy.

VERNON WATKINS

Beethoven's Death Mask

I imagine him still with heavy brow.
Huge, black, with bent head and falling hair,
He ploughs the landscape. His face
Is this hanging mask transfigured,
This mask of death which the white lights make stare.

I see the thick hands clasped; the scare-crow coat;
The light strike upwards at the holes for eyes;
The beast squat in that mouth, whose opening is
The hollow opening of an organ pipe:
There the wind sings and the harsh longing cries.

He moves across my vision like a ship.
What else is iron but he? The fields divide
And, heaving, are changing waters of the sea.
He is prisoned, masked, shut off from Being.
Life, like a fountain, he sees leap — outside.

Yet, in that head there twists the roaring cloud
And coils, as in a shell, the roaring wave.
The damp leaves whisper; bending to the rain
The April rises in him, chokes his lungs
And climbs the torturing passage of his brain.

Then the drums move away, the Distance shows:
Now cloud-hid peaks are bared; the mystic One
Horizons haze, as the blue incense, heaven.
Peace, peace. . . . Then splitting skull and dream, there comes
Blotting our lights, the Trumpeter, the sun.

STEPHEN SPENDER

Eleusis and Beethoven

This was the Temple of the Mysteries
Where hierophants, enrobed in splendour, gave
To thirsting and expectant multitudes
The pledge of deathless life beyond the grave.

Appalled by the capricious eddying
Of their life's stream, they thronged to celebrate
An arcane ritual designed to cheat
The calm impersonal decrees of fate.

Bruised by the cold, hard light of intellect,
The wearisome debate of right and wrong,
They plunged into the matchless certainty
Of spilled blood and of incense and of song.

We also, jaded by distracting strife
And numbed by inexhaustible regrets,
Turn to the Mysteries and come upon
The temple of the posthumous quartets.

The depths of supernatural grief are here,
Suffused with calm, compassionate delight,
And echoes from an ampler world than this
Float through the radiance of the dazzling night.

The pulse of joy vibrates, the holy flame
Burns inextinguishably and provides
Assurance that the questing mind may win
The long-desired salvation that abides

Not in hermetic sacrificial rites,
Or in the chanting of a magic spell,
But in this world, where beauty, sought and found,
Perpetually renews its miracle.

JOHN PRESS

Schubert's Ninth Symphony

Where is the forest, through whose echoing glade
These hollow horns, these horns blowing to lift
The heavy and enamelled leaves which hang
Like tapestry from bole or knotted branch;
Where, printing the virgin soil with golden hooves
A drove of does, white as the unicorn
Dazzle and vanish, as the snow in spring
Unvulnerable still and unafraid?

Who is the huntsman, pausing on the fringe
To raise the horn and blow? Whose is the ear
Which holds the echo, golden as the horn?
The hounds, tawny or dappled like the dark
Fritillary whose livid bell hangs here
By silent waters? Oh, here he stands for ever
Inviting the arrow, the proud, immortal stag
Whose high crown holds the summit of desire.

MARGARET STANLEY-WRENCH

Chopin in London

Guildhall, London, November 16, 1848: 'The people hot from
dancing who went into the room where he played were but little
in the humour to pay attention and anxious to return to their
amusement. He was in the last stages of exhaustion, and the affair
resulted in disappointment. His playing at such a place was a well-
intentioned mistake.'

Poor Fritz, poor Fritzchen, Frédéric Chopin, I
Man my resources to play all the night through,
Flex my wrist as a singer might draw in breath
Pausing before her first irresolute note —

For whom shall I sing but you, old cimbalom,
Simpleton of my wanderings, confidante
Like me played out by circumstance? — slender frame
More or less sound, a few strings snapped inside
Waiting for some Pleyel to refashion them.

Play to yourself, for yourself, while the gay throng
Murmur together, impatient for the end —
It will come, it will come — yellow, shrivelled, cold,
Three layers of flannel under my clothes, still
No bigger than a boy, shrunk over the keys,
Nothing left but my longer-than-ever nose
And a third finger desperately out of play.

Dowagers, dowried debutantes, dowdy belles,
They've got their grip on me — I can't shake them off —
Introduce me all over — who knows to whom? —
Chatter while I perform and then play themselves
Soulful and inaccurate, watching their hands —
Lank dried-up green-and-yellow countesses,
Scottish ladies who whistle to the guitar,
Mrs. Grote, grotesque, with her baritone voice
Asking me up three flights of steps to her box,
We chatted like the goose and the sucking pig
For I could speak no English and she no French —
The continuous round of dinners, concerts, balls,
Surrounded by people, feeling so alone,
More bored than ever, bored, incredibly bored.

If London were not so black, its people dull,
Or if it could lose its smell of soot and fog,
I might even now dare to open my mouth
In this, your so-dear city. But I get up
Coughing myself to death, take soup in my room,
Get Daniel to dress me, gasp all day, not fit
For anything until dinner. Then to stop

At table with these cattle, watching them talk,
Listening to them drink — oh, good kind souls,
So ugly and so alarming, let me breathe,
Understand what is said to me, live to greet
One or two friendly faces — those that are left.

PHILIP HOBSBAUM from Study in a Minor Key

Wagner

O strange awakening to a world of gloom,
And baffled moonbeams and delirious stars,
Of souls that moan behind forbidden bars,
And waving forests swept by wings of doom;

Of heroes falling in unhappy fight,
And wingèd messengers from eyries dim;
And mountains ringed with flame, and shapes that swim
In the deep river's green translucent night.

O restless soul, for ever seeking bliss,
Athirst for ever and unsatisfied,
Whether the woodland starts to the echoing horn,

Or dying Tristan moans by shores forlorn,
Or Siegfried rides through fire to wake his bride,
And shakes the whirling planets with a kiss.

MAURICE BARING

Brahms Peruses the Score of 'Siegfried'

Enormous boots, thick-soled, elastic-sided,
Rest on a carpet shaggy as the pelt
    Of a mountain beast — perhaps
    Is precisely a mountain beast.

The chair adjoining, being unoccupied,
Reveals its antimacassar of scalloped lace
    Like the lower half
    Of a bikini of our day.

The frock-coat is disposed in folds as ample
As those of saints' robes in Renaissance painting:
    The pants, large cylinders
    Of a more recent art.

The background is a dark and shining wealth
Of gilt-tooled books, mahogany, and frames
    For photographs — for this,
    Eventually, no doubt.

The peering old man holds the little score so close
His white beard sweeps the page; but gives no sign
    That he perceives — or smells —
    Anything untoward.

He could not be expected to be thinking
That the legend of courage, kiss and sword arose
    From those atrocious Huns
    Who ruined an empire's comfort.

But how can he not be falling back aghast
At the chromatic spectrum of decay,
    Starting to destroy already
    His classical universe?

ROY FULLER

Fauré

Take me aboard your barque, where the valuable water
   Mirrors the perfect passage of the dove.
Over the glittering gulf the sun burns whiter
   The charts of envy and the reefs of love.

Lost in the frosty light the desperate hunter
   Hurls his black horn-note on the wrecked château
Where in despair the signalman of winter
   Winds on its walls the flashing flags of snow.

I see (captured my caravel) the stolen city
   Falling like Falcon to the cunning bay.
The holy sea, unmerciful and mighty,
   Strides with the tide its penance all the day.

Fling like a king your coin on the clear passage
   Bribing the sea-guard and the stumbling gun.
On the salt lawn scribble your last message
   Rallying the rout of ice on the storming sun.

CHARLES CAUSLEY

Liadov: 'The Enchanted Lake'

The sheer stillness of the water, that resembles,
Under the white sky, a sheet of frosted glass,
Through bare, black boughs, the spring's deserted temples,
Aches with a silent glitter in the lonely pass.

Time, deafened by the cold, in flakes as thin as ash
Prints weightless tracks. Pale distances like muted cymbals
Now clash into nothingness, now tingle, with a flash
Of ice, in dark groves where a fountain leaps and stumbles.

The crystal water creaks and shimmers, grumbles
For summer's departed doves. But out of black trees, a white
    stag
Bears crowns of antlers, breaking dead thickets, tangles
Spiked with rime; and pauses, faint breath drifting like a flag.

On harmless feet, and bearing, like a ghost, a sprig
Of first spring leaves; bending his antlered brows, he tramples
With delicate and magic hoof, earth's icy crag.
And swans, released, move down the lake, that wakes, and
    trembles.

JAMES KIRKUP

Edward Elgar (1857–1934)

I

A boy among the reeds on Severn shore
Sound-bathing: a ghost humming his 'cello tune
Upon the Malvern hills: and in between,
Mostly enigma. Who shall read this score?

The stiff, shy, blinking man in a norfolk suit:
The martinet: the gentle-minded squire:
The piano-tuner's son from Worcestershire:
The Edwardian grandee: how did they consort

In such luxuriant themes? Not privilege
Nor talent's cute, obsequious ear attuned
His soul to the striding rhythms, the unimpugned
Melancholy of a vulgar, vivid age.

Genius alone can move by singular ways
Yet home to the heart of all, the common chord;
Beat to its own time, timelessly make heard
A long-breathed statement or a hesitant phrase.

For me, beyond the marches of his pride,
Through the dark airs and rose-imperial themes,
A far West-country summer glares and glooms,
A boy calls from the reeds on Severn side.

II

Orchards are in it — the vale of Evesham blooming:
Rainshine of orchards blowing out of the past.
The sadness of remembering orchards that never bore,
Never for us bore fruit: year after year they fruited
But all, all was premature —
We were not ripe to gather the full beauty.
And now when I hear 'orchards' I think of loss, recall
White tears of blossom streaming away downwind,
And wish the flower could have stayed to be one with the fruit
    it formed.
Oh, coolness at the core of early summers,
Woodwind haunting those green expectant alleys,
Our blossom falling, falling.

Hills are in it — the Malverns, Bredon, Cotswold.
A meadowsweetness of high summer days:
Clovering bees, time-honeyed bells, the lark's top C.
Hills where each sound, like larksong, passes into light,
And light is music all but seen.
Dawn's silvery tone and evening's crimson adagio;
Noonday on the full strings of sunshine simmering, dreaming,
No past, no future, the pulse of time unnoticed:
Cloud-shadows sweeping in arpeggios up the hillsides;
Grey, muted light which, brooding on stone, tree, clover
And cornfield, makes their colours sing most clear —
All moods and themes of light.

And a river — call it the Severn — a flowing-awayness.
Bray of moonlight on water; brassy flamelets
Of marigold, buttercup, flag-iris in water-meadows;

Kingfishers, mayflies, mills, regattas: the ever-rolling
Controlled percussion of thunderous weirs.
Rivers are passionate gods: they flood, they drown,
Roar themselves hoarse, ripple to gaiety, lull the land
With slow movements of tender meditation.
And in it too, in his music, I hear the famous river —
Always and never the same, carrying far
Beyond our view, reach after noble reach —
That bears its sons away.

C. DAY LEWIS

For the 90th Birthday of Sibelius, December 8, 1955

You are the old, the violent and melancholy master of that final
    land,
Where, down the sky's large whitenesses, the archipelagoes of
    day
Gradually move, on forests light with birch and black with larch,
In grave progressions, all the silent masses of the hanging snows.

There the ancestral stillness pulses with the beat of high
Oceans hammering unalterable shores, and shivers with leagues
Of light-sheeted lakes baring their wide reflections to a wind
That greys their elemental pallor with the dark of stone.

A land of quiet marches, where the estuaries of the constant day
Spread vast, ethereal and cold in the remoteness of the sun,
And air teems with the waterfalling shade of clouds and wings;
A land of mysterious natural sounds and thunderous pauses.

Here muted horns blow sharp and small as human cries
Over the ground of ocean, over the groined land brooding in
    male
Slumber. Under the generating spells of ice and sand
Firm winter holds in moody restlessness the seed

Of rock and iron, the fertile germ of energy, abundant, wild.
All quivers in the drum-deep thrall, the whispering suspension
Of supernatural breath: a poised avalanche trembles on a thrust-
    ing root
That groans and rustles in the dark, whose trumpet splits the
    cataracts of sleep.

Now a distant horse and rider flicker through the running trees;
A hero stirs, and tramples the ice along the river's edge. In mid
Night, men and horses lean to the festive ploughs;
Black boughs dance with birds, and the birds are leaves.

— May you, too, austere and stern and legendary master,
Feel always in the age of earth the gathering Spring,
And see the new leaves lifted on a flight of swans,
And hear again the music of the air, the ocean and the earth

Release their gay eternities from grief and wrong —
And let the Winter move you always with its hidden song.

JAMES KIRKUP

FANCIES AND
FANTASIES

The Fancy Concert

They talked of their concerts, and singers, and scores,
And pitied the fever that kept me indoors;
And I smiled in my thought, and said, 'O ye sweet fancies,
And animal spirits, that still in your dances
Come bringing me visions to comfort my care,
Now fetch me a concert — in paradise air.'

Then a wind, like a storm out of Eden, came pouring
Fierce into my room, and made tremble the flooring;
And filled with a sudden impetuous trample
Of heaven, its corners; and swelled it to ample
Dimensions to breathe in, and space for all power;
Which falling as suddenly, lo! the sweet flower
Of an exquisite fairy-voice opened its blessing;
And ever and aye, to its constant addressing,
There came, falling in with it, each in the last,
Flageolets, one by one, and flutes blowing more fast,
And hautboys and clarinets, acrid of reed,
And the violin, smoothlier sustaining the speed
As the rich tempest gathered, and busy ringing moons
Of tambours, and huge basses, and giant bassoons;
And the golden trombone, that darteth its tongue
Like a bee of the gods; nor was absent the gong,
Like a sudden, fate-bringing, oracular sound,
Of earth's iron genius, burst up from the ground,
A terrible slave, come to wait on his masters
The gods with exultings that clang like disasters,
And then spoke the organs, the very gods they,
Like thunders that roll on a wind-blowing day;
And taking the rule of the roar in their hands,
Lo, the Genii of Music came out of all lands;
And one of them said, 'Will my lord tell his slave,
What concert 'twould please his Firesideship to have?'

Then I said in a tone of immense will and pleasure,
'Let orchestras rise to some exquisite measure;
And let there be lights and be odours; and let
The lovers of music serenely be set;
And then with their singers in lily-white stoles,
And themselves clad in rose-colour, fetch me the souls
Of all the composers accounted divinest,
And with their own hands, let them play me their finest.'

And lo! was performed with immense will and pleasure,
And orchestras rose to an exquisite measure;
And lights were about me, and odours, and set
Were the lovers of music all wondrously met;
And then, with their singers in lily-white stoles,
And themselves clad in rose-colour, in came the souls
Of all the composers accounted divinest,
And, with their own hands, did they play me their finest.

Oh, truly, was Italy heard then and Germany,
Melody's heart, and the rich brain of harmony;
Pure Paisiello, whose airs are as new,
Though we know them by heart, as May blossoms and dew;
And Nature's twin son, Pergolesi; and Bach,
Old father of Fugues, with his endless fine talk;
And Gluck, who saw gods; and the learned sweet feeling
Of Handel; and Winter, whose sorrows are healing;
And gentlest Corelli, whose bowing seems made
For a hand with a jewel; and Handel arrayed
In Olympian thunders, vast lord of the spheres,
Yet pious himself, with his blindness in tears,
A lover withal, and a conqueror, whose marches
Bring demi-gods under victorious arches;
Then Arne, sweet and tricksome; and masterly Purcell,
Lay-clerical soul; and Mozart universal,
But chiefly with exquisite gallantries found,
With a grove in the distance of holier sound;

Chamber Concert

Nor forgot was thy dulcitude, loving Sacchini;
Nor love, young or dying, in shape of Bellini;
Nor Weber, nor Himmel, nor mirth's sweetest name
Cimarosa; much less the great agan-voiced fame
Of Marcello, that hushed the Venetian sea;
And strange was the shout, when it wept, hearing thee
Thou soul full of grace as of grief, my heart-cloven,
My poor, my most rich, my all-feeling Beethoven.

O'er all, like a passion, great Pasta[1] was heard,
As high as her heart, that truth—uttering bird;
And Banti[2] was there; and Grassini,[3] that goddess!
Dark, deep-toned, large, lovely, with glorious bodice;
And Mara;[4] and Malibran,[5] stung to the tips
Of her fingers with pleasure; and rich Fodor's[6] lips;
And manly in voice as in tone, Augrisani;[7]
And Naldi,[8] thy whim; and thy grace, Tramezzani;[9]
And was it a voice, or what was it? Say
That like a fallen angel beginning to pray,
Was the soul of all tears and celestial despair?
Paganini it was, 'twixt his dark flowing hair.
So now we had instrument, now we had song;
Now chorus, a thousand-voiced, one-hearted throng;
Now pauses that pampered resumption, and now —
But who shall describe what was played us, or how?
'Twas wonder, 'twas transport, humility, pride;
'Twas the heart of the mistress that sat by one's side;
'Twas the graces invisible moulding the air
Into all that is shapely, and lovely and fair;
And running our fancies their tenderest rounds
Of endearments and luxuries, turned into sounds,

---

[1] Italian soprano, 1798–1865   [2] Italian soprano, 1756–1806   [3] Italian
contralto, 1773–1850   [4] German soprano, 1749–1833   [5] Spanish mezzo-
contralto, 1808–1836   [6] French soprano, 1789–1870   [7] Dates unknown
[8] Italian baritone, 1770–1820   [9] Dates unknown

'Twas argument even, the logic of tones;
'Twas memory, 'twas wishes, 'twas laughter, 'twas moans;
'Twas pity and love, in pure impulse obeyed;
'Twas the breath of the stuff of which passion is made.

And these are the concerts I have at my will;
Then dismiss them, and patiently think of your 'bill'.
Aside. Yet Lablache, after all, makes me long to go, still.

LEIGH HUNT

Paganini

Ceilings of knobbled gold
almost flew apart;
glass pagoda chandeliers
rocked as thousands
of frilled palms
hammered in pairs
for he paused — the rosewood
shrank to a gutted box,
with inky date and name
on a label inside.

Urchin and cat, before dawn,
heard heavenly scratchings,
underground, as they ran
for oven and fish.
Horrible cries
under the grill!
From a cellar little evidenced
by the one candle,
came shrieks to appal
the running thief.

CHRISTOPHER MIDDLETON

Epitaph upon Master Parsons,[1] Organist at Westminster

Death passing by and hearing Parsons play,
Stood much amazed at his depth of skill,
And said 'This artist must with me away,'
For Death bereaves us of the better skill.
   But let the quire, while he keeps time, sing on,
   For Parsons rests, his service being done.

ANON.

Musical Love

Love once would daunce within my Mistris eye,
And wanting musique fitting for the place,
Swore that I should the Instrument supply,
And sodainly presents me with her face:
Straightwayes my pulse playes lively in my vaines,
My panting breath doth keepe a meaner time,
My quav'ring artiers be the Tenours straynes,
My trembling sinewes serve the Counterchime,
My hollow sighs the deepest base doe beare,
True diapazon in distincted sound:
My panting hart the treble makes the ayre,
And descants finely on the musiques ground;
   Thus like a Lute or Violl did I lye,
   Whilst he proud slave daunc'd galliards in her eye.

MICHAEL DRAYTON

[1] Parsons, organist of Westminster Abbey, died in 1623

The Three Musicians

Along the path that skirts the wood,
    The three musicians wend their way,
Pleased with their thoughts, each other's mood,
    Franz Himmel's latest roundelay,
The morning's work, a new-found theme, their breakfast and the
        summer day.

One's a soprano, lightly frocked
    In cool, white muslin that just shows
Her brown silk stockings gaily clocked,
    Plump arms and elbows tipped with rose,
And frills of petticoats and things, and outlines as the warm wind
        blows.

Beside her a slim, gracious boy
    Hastens to mend her tresses' fall,
And dies her favour to enjoy,
    And dies for *reclame* and recall
At Paris and St Petersburg, Vienna and St James's Hall.

The third's a Polish pianist
    With big engagements everywhere,
A light heart and an iron wrist,
    And shocks and shoals of yellow hair,
And fingers that can trill on sixths and fill beginners with despair.

The three musicians stroll along
    And pluck the ears of ripened corn,
Break into odds and ends of song,
    And mock the woods with Siegfried's horn,
And fill the air with Gluck, and fill the tweeded tourist's soul with
        scorn.

The Polish genius lags behind,
    And, with some poppies in his hand,
Picks out the strings and wood and wind
    Of an imaginary band,
Enchanted that for once his men obey his beat and understand.

The charming cantatrice reclines
    And rests a moment where she sees
Her château's roof that hotly shines
    Amid the dusky summer trees,
And fans herself, half shuts her eyes, and smoothes the frock about
    her knees.

The gracious boy is at her feet,
    And weighs his courage with his chance;
His fears soon melt in noonday heat.
    The tourist gives a furious glance,
Red as his guide-book grows, moves on, and offers up a prayer
    for France.

AUBREY BEARDSLEY

O Dowland, Old John Dowland

O Dowland, old John Dowland, make a tune for this,
Two lovers married, like two turtle-doves,
Whose mutual eyes no curtain knew nor shade their kiss
And fruitful with a child their holiday loves.

Set that to harmony and then beside it set
Heaven steeled with armament and nations bent
On conquest and resistance, the unavoided net
Of time still drawn in moment by moment.

Is there for such sorrow and love, Dowland, a tune
In your book? Heavy is it for lute to lift?
Yet must we make our poem of it and on the dune
Of this century scatter our sea-thrift.

HAL SUMMERS

Haydn—Military Symphony

Music creates two grenadiers, scarlet and tall
Leisurely fellows: in the long afternoon
They stroll with royal slow motion. How they twirl
Their regular canes. Each silly servant girl
Regards wide-eyed or diffidently, soon
Is captured quite. The idle lords of all

The park, the dogs, the children, both wheel
Down the long walk between the lazy trees.
Yet scrutinize the regimental pair
And you will find, they are but men of air —
Their summer is a fantasy, and these
Like all authentic heroes are unreal.

Follow them none the less at the same pace:
For you perhaps to step behind these two
May shew such dead romances can revive,
The painted backcloth quicken and be alive.
You will look out upon this painted view
Of madmen in a non-existent place.

KEITH DOUGLAS

After the Concert

Seated in the cafeteria, you say
'Don't you find atonalists can feel things
more intensely?'
Your intellectual gaze is riveted
upon me.
The clink of passing coffee cups,
crumbstrewn table-tops
and atmosphere as abstract
as our desiccated thoughts.

'Than ourselves, you mean?' I say,
though I see I do not know this game
and will not score as high as some
of those around me may.

On the sea of conversations sail the names
Schönberg, Stravinsky, Webern, Berg.

Suddenly you come alive and smile so beautifully
yet mystically
I must have scored and feel so pleased
now your blue eyes and soft blond hair
are pleasantly disposed towards me.

You say,
'Intensity of feeling can really only be really
only be communicated musically atonally absolutely
in fragmented diamond bright thoughts transmitted
purely I mean musically atonally realistically in
terms of abstract sound.'
Your golden skin, I think, is not for thoughts like these
and dream of you and me embracing by the sea
where little boats so proudly show their names —
Schönberg, Stravinsky, Webern, Berg.

You say,
'At any rate the romantics killed music its meaning
and all its purity it is a period I would rather forget.'
Then, I think, with the music I am killed and look
ashamed into your eyes and dare not say
I loved you and
Schönberg, Stravinsky, Webern, Berg.

DAVID STAPLETON

The First Harp-player

It will not matter
Says the first harp-player,
What string I pluck, I
Shall not waken her.

For she is tired of music,
Since the grey musician
Played his cold rebbeck for her
As only he can.

Break, like spent bubbles,
My notes! Shatter and tumble!
She was light, she was swift, she was lovely,
And now she must crumble.

HUMBERT WOLFE

On a Portrait of Mme Rimsky-Korsakov

Serene, not as a prize for conflict won,
But mark of never having had to fight,
Needing no mind, because too beautiful,
She sat embodying her unconcern
For all charades of love or symbolism.
  Nicholas was inspecting a brass band,
  Driving to lunch with Borodin and Cui,
  Checking the full score of *The Snow Maiden*.

That dateless look, impersonal above
The coarse placing of the heart's Hollywood,
Writes off poor Janey Morris as a paddler
In joy and agony, a pop-eyed clown
Skinny and thick-lipped with her pomegranate.
  The Snow Maiden and the rest of the stuff
  Attain the permanence of print, wax, and
  Footnotes in treatises on orchestration.

KINGSLEY AMIS

The Child Musician

He had played for his lordship's levee,
   He had played for her ladyship's whim,
Till the poor little head was heavy,
   And the poor little brain would swim.

And the face grew peaked and eerie,
   And the large eyes strange and bright,
And they said — too late — 'He is weary!
   He shall rest for, at least, to-night!'

But at dawn, when the birds were waking,
   As they watched in the silent room,
With the sound of a strained cord breaking,
   A something snapped in the gloom.

'Twas a string of his violoncello,
   And they heard him stir in his bed: —
'Make room for a tired little fellow,
   King God!' — was the last that he said.

AUSTIN DOBSON

WIT, HUMOUR AND RIGHTEOUS INDIGNATION

Free Thoughts on Several Eminent Composers

Some cry up Haydn, some Mozart,
Just as the whim bites; for my part,
I do not care a farthing candle
For either of them, or for Handel.
Cannot a man live free and easy,
Without admiring Pergolesi?
Or thro' the world with comfort go,
That never heard of Doctor Blow?
So help me God, I hardly have;
And yet I eat, and drink, and shave,
Like other people, if you watch it,
And know no more of Stave or Crotchet,
Than did the primitive Peruvians;
Or those old ante-queer-Diluvians
That lived in the unwash'd world with Tubal,
Before that dirty blacksmith Jubal
By stroke on anvil, or by summ'at,
Found out, to his great surprise, the gamut.
I care no more for Cimarosa,
Than he did for Salvator Rosa,
Being no painter; and bad luck
Be mine, if I can bear that Gluck!
Old Tycho Brahe, and modern Herschel,
Had something in 'em; but who's Purcell?
The devil, with his foot so cloven,
For aught I care, may take Beethoven;
And, if the bargain does not suit,
I'll throw him Weber in to boot.
There's not the splitting of a splinter
To chuse 'twixt him last named, and Winter.
Of Doctor Pepusch old queen Dido
Knew just as much, God knows, as I do.
I would not go four miles to visit

Sebastian Bach (or Batch, which is it?);
No more I would for Bononcini.
As for Novello, or Rossini,
I shall not say a word to grieve 'em,
Because they're living; so I leave 'em.

CHARLES LAMB

Lamb's sister Mary later wrote to Vincent Novello:—

The reason why my brother's so severe,
Vincentio, is — my brother has no *ear*;
And Caradori her melifluous throat
Might stretch in vain to make him learn a note.
Of common tunes he knows not anything,
Not *Rule Britannia* from *God Save the King*.
He rail at Handel! He the gamut quiz!
I'd lay my life he knows not what it is.
His spite of music is a pretty whim —
He loves it not because it loves not him.

Epigram on Handel and Bononcini

Some say, compar'd to *Bononcini*
That Mynheer *Handel's* but a Ninny;
Others aver, that he to *Handel*
Is scarcely fit to hold a *Candle*.
Strange all this Difference should be
'Twixt Tweedle-*dum* and Tweedle-*dee*!

JOHN BYROM

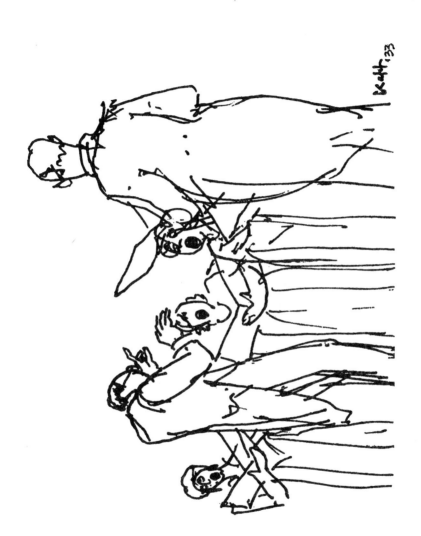

Foreign Songsters

In Days of Old, when *Englishmen* were — Men,
Their Musick, like themselves, was grave and plain;
The manly Trumpets, and the simple Reed,
Alike with *Citizen* and *Swain* agreed;
Whose Songs, in lofty Sense, but humble Verse,
Their Loves and Wars alternately rehearse;
Sung by themselves, their homely Cheer to crown,
In Tunes from Sire to Son deliver'd down.

But now, since *Britains* are become polite,
Since Few can *read*, and Fewer still can *write*;
Since Trav'ling has so much improv'd our Beaux,
That each brings home a foreign *Tongue*, or — *Nose*;
And Ladies paint with that amazing Grace,
That their best *Vizard* is their natural *Face*;
Since *South-Sea Schemes* have so inrich'd the Land,
That *Footmen* 'gainst their *Lords* for *Boroughs* stand;
Since *Masquerades* and *Op'ras* made their Entry,
And *Heydegger*[1] reign'd *Guardian* of our Gentry;
A hundred various Instruments combine,
And foreign *Songsters* in the Concert join:
The *Gallick Horn,* whose sounding Tube in vain
Pretends to emulate the *Trumpet's* Strain;
The *shrill-ton'd Fiddle,* and the *warbling Flute,*
The *grave Bassoon, deep Base,* and *tinkling Lute,*
The *jingling Spinnet,* and the *full-mouth'd Drum,*
A *Roman Capon,* and *Venetian Strum,*
All league, melodious Nonsense to dispense,
And give us *Sound,* and *Show,* instead of *Sense*;
In unknown Tongues mysterious Dullness chant,
Make Love in *Tune,* or *thro' the Gamut* rant.

JAMES MILLER

---

[1] Heydegger (1659?-1749), manager of the opera at the Haymarket
Theatre, was for a time in partnership with Handel

Sonata

Who's that with roses and with laurels crowned,
The guest of princes and the banquet's vaunt,
With whose applause the capitals resound?
This is the brilliant executant.

And who is this, obscure, ill, poor, and old,
For every prize a gambler and a loser,
Friendless, despised, who scribbles in the cold
Attic at nightfall? That is the composer.

HAL SUMMERS

The Organist in Heaven

When Wesley died, the Angelic Orders,
    To see him at the state,
Pressed so incontinent that the warders
    Forgot to shut the gate.
So I, that hitherto had followed
    As one with grief o'ercast,
Where for the doors a space was hollowed,
    Crept in, and heard what passed.
And God said: — 'Seeing thou hast given
    Thy life to my great sounds,
Choose thou through all the cirque of Heaven
    What most of bliss redounds.'
Then Wesley said: 'I hear the thunder
    Low growling from Thy seat —
Grant me that I may bind it under
    The trampling of my feet.'

And Wesley said: 'See, lightning quivers
   Upon the presence walls —
Lord, give me of it four great rivers,
   To be my manuals.'
And then I saw the thunder chidden
   As slave to his desire;
And then I saw the space bestridden
   With four great bands of fire;
And stage by stage, stop stop subtending,
   Each lever strong and true,
One shape inextricable blending,
   The awful organ grew.
Then certain angels clad the Master
   In very marvellous wise,
Till clouds of rose and alabaster
   Concealed him from mine eyes.
And likest to a dove soft brooding,
   The innocent figure ran;
So breathed the breath of his preluding,
   And then the fugue began —
Began, but, to his office turning,
   The porter swung his key;
Wherefore, although my heart was yearning,
   I had to go; but he
Played on; and, as I downward clomb,
   I heard the mighty bars
Of thunder-gusts, that shook Heaven's dome,
   And moved the balanced stars.

T. E. BROWN

On Lutestrings Catt-eaten

Are these the strings that poets feigne
Have clear'd the Ayre, and calm'd the mayne?
Charm'd wolves, and from the mountaine creasts
Made forests dance with all their beasts?
Could these neglected shreads you see
Inspire a Lute of Ivorie
And make it speake? Oh! think then what
Hath beene committed by my catt,
Who, in the silence of this night
Hath gnawne these cords, and marr'd them quite;
Leaving such reliques as may be
For fretts,[1] not for my lute, but me.
Pusse, I will curse thee; may'st thou dwell
With some dry Hermit in a cell
Where Ratt neere peep'd, where mouse neere fedd,
And flyes goe supperlesse to bedd;
Or with some close-par'd Brother,[2] where
Thou'lt fast each Saboath in the yeare;
Or else, prophane, be hang'd on Munday,
For butchering a mouse on Sunday;
Or May'st thou tumble from some tower,
And misse to light upon all fower,
Taking a fall that may untie
Eight of nine lives, and let them flye;
Or may the midnight embers sindge
Thy daintie coate, or Jane beswinge
Thy hide, when she shall take thee biting
Her cheese clouts, or her house beshiting.
What, was there neere a ratt nor mouse,
Nor Buttery ope? nought in the house

[1] a play on the two meanings of 'fret': as an interlaced pattern and as an irritation
[2] closely shorn Puritan

178

But harmelesse Lutestrings could suffice
Thy paunch, and draw thy glaring eyes?
Did not thy conscious stomach finde
Nature prophan'd, that kind with kind
Should stanch his hunger? thinke on that,
Thou caniball, and Cyclops catt.
For know, thou wretch, that every string
Is a catt-gutt, which art doth spinne
Into a thread; and how suppose
Dunstan, that snuff'd the divell's nose,
Should bid these strings revive, as once
He did the calfe, from naked bones;
Or I, to plague thee for thy sinne,
Should draw a circle, and beginne
To conjure, for I am, look to 't,
An Oxford scholler, and can doo 't.
Then with three setts of mapps and mowes,
Seaven of odd words, and motley showes,
A thousand tricks, that may be taken
From Faustus, Lambe, or Fryar Bacon:
I should beginne to call my strings
My catlings, and my mynikins;
And they recalled, straight should fall
To mew, to purr, to catterwaule
From puss's belly. Sure as death,
Pusse should be an Engastranith;
Pusse should be sent for to the king
For a strange bird, or some rare thing.
Pusse should be sought to farre and neere,
As she some cunning woman were.
Pusse should be carried up and downe,
From shire to shire, from Towne to Towne,
Like to the camell, Leane as Hagg,
The Elephant, or Apish negg,
For a strange sight; pusse should be sung
In Lousy Ballads, midst the Throng

At markets, with as good a grace
As Agincourt, or Chevy-chase.
The Troy-sprung Brittan would forgoe
His pedigree he chaunteth soe,
And singe that Merlin — long deceast —
Returned is in a nyne-liv'd beast.
    Thus, pusse, thou seest what might betyde thee;
But I forbeare to hurt or chide thee;
For may be pusse was melancholy
And so to make her blythe and jolly,
Finding these strings, shee'ld have a fitt
Of mirth; nay, pusse, if that were it,
Thus I revenge mee, that as thou
Hast played on them, I've plaid on you;
And as thy touch was nothing fine,
Soe I've but scratch'd these notes of mine.

THOMAS MASTER

A Musical Instrument

What was he doing, the great god Pan,
    Down in the reeds by the river?
Spreading ruin and scattering ban,
Splashing and paddling with hoofs of a goat,
And breaking the golden lilies afloat
    With the dragon-fly on the river.

He tore out a reed, the great god Pan,
    From the deep cool bed of the river:
The limpid water turbidly ran,
And the broken lilies a-dying lay,
And the dragon-fly had fled away,
    Ere he brought it out of the river.

High on the shore sate the great god Pan,
  While turbidly flowed the river;
And hacked and hewed as a great god can,
With his hard bleak steel at the patient reed,
Till there was not a sign of a leaf indeed
  To prove it fresh from the river.

He cut it short, did the great god Pan
  (How tall it stood in the river!),
Then drew the pith, like the heart of a man,
Steadily from the outside ring,
And notched the poor dry empty thing
  In holes, as he sate by the river.

'This is the way,' laughed the great god Pan
  (Laughed while he sate by the river),
'The only way, since gods began
To make sweet music, they could succeed.'
Then, dropping his mouth to a hole in the reed,
  He blew in power by the river.

Sweet, sweet, sweet, O Pan!
  Piercing sweet by the river!
Blinding sweet, O great god Pan!
The sun on the hill forgot to die,
And the lilies revived, and the dragon-fly
  Came back to dream on the river.

Yet half a beast is the great god Pan,
  To laugh as he sits by the river,
Making a poet out of a man:
The true gods sigh for the cost and pain, —
For the reed which grows nevermore again
  As a reed with the reeds in the river.

ELIZABETH BARRETT BROWNING

The Old Orange Flute
(to the tune of 'Villikens and his Dinah')

In the County Tyrone, in the town of Dungannon,
Where many a ruction myself had a han' in,
Bob Williamson lived, a weaver by trade.
And all of us thought him a stout Orange blade.
On the Twelfth of July as around it would come
Bob played on the flute to the sound of the drum;
You may talk of your harp, your piano or lute,
But there's nothing compared with the old Orange flute.

But Bob the deceiver he took us all in,
For he married a Papish called Brigid McGinn,
Turned Papish himself, and forsook the old cause
That gave us our freedom, religion, and laws.
Now the boys of the place made some comment upon it,
And Bob had to fly to the Province of Connacht,
He fled with his wife and his fixings to boot,
And along with the latter his old Orange flute.

At the chapel on Sundays, to atone for past deeds,
He said *Paters* and *Aves* and counted his beads,
Till after some time, at the priest's own desire,
He went with his old flute to play in the choir.
He went with his old flute to play for the Mass,
And the instrument shivered and sighed: 'Oh, alas!'
And blow as he would, though it made a great noise,
The flute would play only *The Protestant Boys*.

Bob jumped, and he started, and got in a flutter,
And threw his old flute in the best Holy Water;
He thought that this charm would bring some other sound;
When he blew it again, it played *'Croppies'*[1] *lie down*;

[1] 'Croppies' refers to the rebels of 1798 who cut their hair short in
sympathy with the French Revolution

And for all he could whistle, and finger, and blow,
To play Papish music he found it no go;
Kick the Pope, The Boyne Water, it freely would sound,
But one Papish squeak in it couldn't be found.

At a council of priests that was held the next day,
They decided to banish the old flute away
For they couldn't knock heresy out of its head
And they bought Bob a new one to play in its stead.
So the old flute was doomed and its fate was pathetic,
'Twas fastened and burned at the stake as heretic,
While the flames roared around it they heard a strange noise —
'Twas the old flute still whistling *The Protestant Boys*.

ANON.

Knew the Master

You knew the Master. Come and talk about him
And we'll uncork a bottle, maybe two.
He used to write in bed in a red nightcap,
Or so the legend goes. And is it true
He played the harpsichord with both eyes shut?
Tell us about that scandalous affair
That set him working on the great quartets.
They say the Princess had a private stair.
You were his pupil and amanuensis —
You must have heard. What's that? You'd like to play
Some recent compositions of your own?
Well, not just now, perhaps some other day.

JAMES REEVES

Facing the Music

We who love music are not pretty.
    Dear me, no!
Though there be cherished in each hidden heart
The selfsame beauties which inspired Mozart
    Our bodies singularly fail to show
      them. It's a pity.

    In concert halls we slump into our places,
      hair awry.
Feeling in perfect sympathy with Brahms,
We yet but manifest the doubtful charms
    of troglodytes. I wonder why
      we have *such* faces!

    Nothing matches. We will wear goloshes,
      baggy coats,
strive all in vain to emulate Miss Sitwell
in gowns which should but do not fit well,
    while over us there languorously floats
      the smell of mackintoshes.

    We who love music are not pretty.
      And since our souls
Are spun about with sweet melodious notes,
Why have we bulging brows and pendant throats,
    and downy lips and podgy hands and moles?
      It's such a pity!

VIRGINIA GRAHAM

Miss Multitude at the Trombone

If trombone music be the food of love,
   Play on, Miss Multitude, assuage my hunger,
Nor heed the tale, my brawny turtle-dove,
   Of Mrs Relf, divorced by a fishmonger.
Thou wert not born to burst, immortal bird,
   Though gales of breath may shake thy massive frame.
Heard melodies are sweet; leave those unheard
   To instruments which daintier mouths may tame.
Follow thy vision, laboriously pursued
   From blast to blast. Play on, Miss Multitude.

J. B. MORTON

The Musician to his Love

Sing me no song! Give me one silent hour!
   Your nerve is strong, but mine's a fragile flower;
Sing when I'm far from here, say in Hong Kong;
   But, if you love me, dear, sing me no song.

When I the prelude played, and bade you sing,
   Oh! the strange noise we made! The jangling!
White notes I found were wrong, so were the black!
   For you had pitched the song right in the crack!

If you were dumb, and not a single note
   Could ever come from out that rounded throat,
Songs you might spell on finger and on thumb,
   Oh, I could love you well if you were dumb!

If I were deaf, oh! then I'd let you sing
    In C or F, and watch the guests take wing;
I'd let thee shriek and yell above the treble clef,
    That would not break the spell — if I were deaf!

You have no ear — no ear for tune or rhyme,
    And, it is very clear, no sense of time.
Sing to my wealthy aunt, her nerves are strong,
    But, if it's me you want — sing me no song!

PERCY FRENCH

The Music of the Future

The politest musician that ever was seen
Was Montague Meyerbeer Mendelssohn Green.
So extremely polite he would take off his hat
Whenever he chanced to meet with a cat.

'It's not that I'm partial to cats,' he'd explain;
'Their music to me is unspeakable pain.
There's nothing that causes my flesh so to crawl
As when they perform a G-flat caterwaul.

'Yet I cannot help feeling — in spite of their din —
When I hear at a concert the first violin
Interpret some exquisite theme of my own,
If it were not for *cat gut* I'd never be known.

'And so, when I bow, as you see, to a cat,
It isn't to *her* that I take off my hat;
But to fugues and sonatas that possibly hide
Uncomposed in her — well — in her tuneful inside.'

OLIVER HERFORD

INDEX OF FIRST LINES

187

Lips hardened by winter's dumb duress, 53
Love once would daunce within my Mistris eye, 160

Many love music but for music's sake, 18
Marvellous music laps me round, 126
Music comes, 27
Music divine, proceeding from above, 36
Music creates two grenadiers, scarlet and tall, 164
Music, dear solace to my thoughts neglected, 26
Music to hear, why hear'st thou music sadly? 25
My brides are ravished away, are ravished away, 110
My heart 's an old Spinet with strings, 31

No, Music, thou art not the 'food of Love', 13
Nor cold, nor stern, my soul! yet I detest, 29
Now is the focus of all hopes, 78

O Dowland, old John Dowland, make a tune for this, 163
O strange awakening to a world of gloom, 146
Of sundry sorts that were, as the musician likes, 114
Oh friend, whom glad or grave we seek, 128
On these ancient disks, smooth-backed, severe, 56

Play the tune again; but this time, 44
Poor Fritz, poor Fritzchen, Frédéric Chopin, I, 144

Remote in the dream perspective of the street, 58

Seated in the cafeteria, you say, 165
Seated one day at the organ, 100
Serene, not as a prize for conflict won, 167
Simply one warm night, among much warmth and many nights, 62
Since Musick so delights the Sense, 120
Sing me no song! Give me one silent hour!, 185
Softly, in the dusk, a woman is singing to me, 32
Some cry up Haydn, some Mozart, 171
Some say, compar'd to Bononcini, 172
So music flowed for them, and left, 40
Speak to us, Music, for the discord jars, 22

Strangely assorted, the shape of song and the bloody man, 60
Sunday gardening, hoeing, trying to think of nothing but, 39
Sweet clavichord, 127
Sweetest of sweets, I thank you when displeasure, 83
Swim with the stream! Sleep as you swim! Let the wave take you! 36

Take me aboard your barque, where the valuable water, 148
That same first fiddler who leads the orchestra tonight, 67
The audience pricks an intellectual Ear, 75
The beat and beat and growl of the Basie band, 61
The chatter thins, lights dip, and dusty crimson, 107
The fiddler knows what's brewing, 65
The fur-cloaked boyars plotting in the hall, 104
The Harpe is an instrumente of sweet melodye, 113,
The lovers have poisoned themselves and died singing, 103
The new moon hangs like an ivory bugle, 8
The politest musician that ever was seen, 186
The sheer stillness of the water, that resembles, 148
The sunshine, and the grace of falling rain, 139
They are gathering round, 63
They often haunt me, these substantial ghosts, 97
They talked of their concerts, and singers, and scores, 155
This is the prettiest motion, 49
This music which you made, Domenico, 136
This was the Temple of the Mysteries, 143
Thirty years ago lying awake, 55
To his sweet lute Apollo sung the motions of the spheres, 24
Tom sang for joy and Ned sang for joy, 51
Trees crept into church, 95

Up in his loft the shy FRCO, 99

We poets pride ourselves on what, 13
We who love music are not pretty, 184
What an enchanted world is this, 31
What fingers plucked these long untroubled strings? 124
What, have the gods their consort sent from heaven, 23
What helps it those, 14
What pale, Victorian invalid, obsessed, 60

What was he doing, the great god Pan, 180
When lo! a harlot form soft sliding by, 108
When music sounds, gone is the earth I know, 4
When the last note is played and void the hall, 3
When to the music of Byrd or Tallis, 83
When thro' life unblest we rove, 19
When Wesley died, the Angelic Orders, 176
When whispering strains do softly steal, 11
Where griping griefs the heart would wound, 9
Where is the forest, through whose echoing glade, 144
While my young cheek retains its healthful hues, 48
Who finds for Figaro's sake, 141
Who's that with roses and with laurels crowned, 176
With what attentive courtesy he bent, 53

Ye sacred Muses, race of Jove, 33
You are the old, the violent and melancholy master of that final land, 151
You knew the Master. Come and talk about him, 183

INDEX TO POETS

ACKNOWLEDGEMENTS

I wish to thank the undermentioned, who have kindly given permission for copyright material to be included. Every effort has been made to trace copyright owners; I apologise in advance to anyone omitted inadvertently.

KINGSLEY AMIS — from *A Look Round the Estate*, Jonathan Cape Ltd. E. N. DA C. ANDRADE — from *Poems and Songs*, Macmillan and Co, the author. W. H. AUDEN — from *Collected Shorter Poems*, 1927–1957, Faber and Faber Ltd, the author. MAURICE BARING — from *The Collected Poems of Maurice Baring*, William Heinemann Ltd, A. P. Watt & Son, the Trustees of the Estate of the late Maurice Baring. MARTIN BELL — from *Collected Poems 1937–1966*, Macmillan and Co., the author. CHARLES CAUSLEY — from *Union Street*, Rupert Hart-Davis Ltd, David Higham Associates. RICHARD CHURCH — from *Collected Poems* and *The Burning Bush*, William Heinemann Ltd. ROBERT CONQUEST — from *Between Mars and Venus*, Hutchinson and Co. JULIAN COOPER — the author. FRANCES CORNFORD — from *On a Calm Shore*, Cresset Press. W. H. DAVIES — from *The Complete Poems of W. H. Davies*, Jonathan Cape Ltd, Mrs H. M. Davies. AUSTIN DOBSON — from *Poetical Works of Austin Dobson*, Oxford University Press. KEITH DOUGLAS — from *Collected Poems*, Faber and Faber Ltd. D. J. ENRIGHT — from *The Laughing Hyena*, Routledge and Kegan Paul Ltd. JOHN FREEMAN — from *Collected Poems*, Macmillan and Co, A. D. Peters and Co. PERCY FRENCH — from *Prose, Poems and Parodies*, The Talbot Press, the Misses E. and J. Percy-French. ROY FULLER — from *Buff*, Andre Deutsch Ltd. VIRGINIA GRAHAM — from *Consider the Years*, Jonathan Cape Ltd, the Proprietors of *Punch*. GEORGE ROSTREVOR HAMILTON — from *Collected Poems*, William Heinemann Ltd. THOMAS HARDY — from *The Collected Poems of Thomas Hardy*, Macmillan and Co,

William Heinemann Ltd, the author. ALASTAIR REID — from *Passwords*, Weidenfeld and Nicholson Ltd. A. L. ROWSE — from *Poems Chiefly Cornish*, Faber and Faber Ltd. SIEGFRIED SASSOON — from *Collected Poems*, Faber and Faber Ltd. SACHEVERELL SITWELL — David Higham Associates. STEPHEN SPENDER — from *Collected Poems*, Faber and Faber Ltd. SIR J. C. SQUIRE — from *Collected Poems of J. C. Squire*, Macmillan and Co, Mr Raglan Squire. MARGARET STANLEY-WRENCH — from *Envoi, Time and Tide* and *The Fortnightly*, the author. DAVID STAPLETON — the author. HAL SUMMERS — from *Hinterland* and *Smoke After Flame*, J. M. Dent and Sons. ARTHUR SYMONS — from *Collected Poems*, William Heinemann Ltd. NATHANIEL TARN — from *Old Savage, Young City*, Jonathan Cape Ltd. A. S. J. TESSIMOND — from *Voices in a Giant City*, William Heinemann Ltd, Hubert Nicholson. R. S. THOMAS — from *Tares*, Rupert Hart-Davis Ltd. EDWARD THOMAS — from *Collected Poems*, Faber and Faber Ltd, Mrs Myfanwy Thomas. W. J. TURNER — from *Selected Poems*, Oxford University Press Ltd, Mrs D. M. Mewton-Wood. VERNON WATKINS — from *The Listener*. LAURENCE WHISTLER — from *The World's Room*, William Heinemann Ltd, and *To Celebrate Her Living*, Rupert Hart-Davis Ltd. HUMBERT WOLFE — from *The Unknown Goddess*, Methuen and Co, Miss Ann Wolfe.